DARE TO
CHANGE
YOUR LIFE

DARE TO
CHANGE
YOUR LIFE

LAWRENCE
OKOLIE

HAPPY
BOOKS
PLACE

Ebury Press an imprint of Ebury Publishing,
20 Vauxhall Bridge Road,
London SW1V 2SA

Ebury Press is part of the Penguin Random House group
of companies whose addresses can be found at
global.penguinrandomhouse.com

First published by Ebury Press in 2021

www.penguin.co.uk

A CIP catalogue record for this book is
available from the British Library

ISBN 9781529109382

Printed and bound in Great Britain by Clays Ltd, Elcograf S.p.A.

The authorised representative in the EEA is
Penguin Random House Ireland, Morrison Chambers,
32 Nassau Street, Dublin D02 YH68

Penguin Random House is committed to a sustainable future for
our business, our readers and our planet. This book is made
from Forest Stewardship Council® certified paper.

For Mum.

CONTENTS

PART 2: YOU'RE GOING TO NEED A PLAN

PART 3: KEEP HUSTLING

FOREWORD

Lawrence and I, we're both from London, and that's how we connect. We also connect on another level: we're both fearless.

As a boxer, you wonder how great you could become, but we both take the approach of saying, 'Let's just get on with it', and feeling no fear.
No matter where we end up, it's going to be better than where we started, in boxing and also in life.
If you're disciplined and you put in a bit of hard work, anything is possible – in my life, in Lawrence's life, and in your life, too.

Lawrence is an inspiration to me and, after reading his story, he'll become an inspiration to you, too (if he wasn't already). I respect and appreciate what he has achieved in boxing. It's always amazing to hear Lawrence's story, and to read it again in these pages, of how he was working in a McDonald's during the 2012 London Olympics but was inspired to become a boxer after watching me fight for a gold medal.

I remember him as an amateur, coming down to my gym, and doing a few rounds. It seemed like a minute after London 2012, Lawrence was boxing with the Olympic guys, and he went on to become an Olympian himself, representing Great Britain at the Rio de Janeiro Games in 2016. Soon after that, he became a professional.

I'm proud to be his friend as well as his manager, mentor and occasional sparring partner.

In Lawrence's first book, you'll get exclusive insight into how he turned his life around and became one of the most inspirational and exciting stories in sport. Lawrence is an honest guy, and it's all in here, with some deeply personal and revealing stories. But, even more importantly, Lawrence's 41 lessons will help you to find your own dream and to turn that into a reality, transforming your own life.

As it says on the front of this book, dare to change your life.

Anthony Joshua

INTRODUCTION

I'm proud of the changes I've made to my life. I've revolutionised my mindset. I've changed how I look at myself and how I look at the world, and I've also improved my lifestyle. Now I want to help you to make changes in your own life.

In the age of Instagram, Twitter and TikTok, I know the power of the printed word. Reading a book can completely transform how someone thinks and acts; books can change lives. That's why I've written this book of life lessons. Currently, there aren't enough black voices in books with inspirational, positive messages, and I'm happy to help address that with *Dare to Change Your Life*. I get huge satisfaction from thinking you'll read my story and be inspired. That would make me feel so blessed. That would be the purest thing. That would make me so happy.

While I'm a fighter, this isn't a boxing memoir purely aimed at fans of the fight game. It's a book with a universal message about living well; that anyone can dare to change their life. Perhaps you're feeling scared, hopeless, and unsure about where you're heading in life and what to do next. Maybe you feel stuck in a job you hate, or a relationship that's going nowhere, and you can't see a way out. Whatever your situation, if you're looking to make changes in your life, I want to help you in these pages. Reading this book is the first step towards daring to change your life.

PART 1
DARE TO CHANGE YOUR LIFE

In these opening chapters, I look at the first steps you need to take to change your life. I'm going to show you that anything is possible, how to find your ambition, and how to believe in yourself when others keep doubting you and your dreams. Among other lessons in this section are why you should always choose being extraordinary over being ordinary, how to keep your focus and avoid being distracted by social media, as well as standing up for yourself, and how a pen and paper are often the best therapy. As you start to make changes, I'll also be urging you not to let impatience kill your dreams.

Anything
is possible

I was nineteen stone, dangerously bloated, clinically obese, and working in McDonald's. I was going nowhere, slowly.

I didn't know it, but I was also just hours away from the moment that would change my life, that would propel me towards the Olympics only four years later. An Olympic cycle that began, in all places, at a burger joint inside Victoria train station, amid the everyday grind and greyness of inner-city London. And which would end in Rio de Janeiro, somewhere between Copacabana Beach and Christ the Redeemer, and surrounded by the world's greatest athletes.

On the way to my shift at McDonald's, I couldn't have predicted that I was about to start my crazy transition from obesity to the Olympics. How could I have foreseen that, when my worldview was framed by the golden arches, and when the closest thing I had to a mentor was Ronald McDonald? And when my boss had just heavily scolded me for turning up only a minute late, which really put a dampener on my mood and my day? If I had ambitions that morning, they weren't to represent Great Britain at the 2016 Olympic Games, and to go on to become a professional boxer. If I aspired to anything, it was to one day become a manager in McDonald's, but after just a year of working there, even that seemed like a distant dream.

My days were measured out in burgers, fries, milkshakes and Happy Meals: the ones I served and the ones I put aside for myself. When I wasn't working in McDonald's, I was eating in McDonald's, several times a day. In between the Big Macs, I was bingeing on bags of Haribo sweets. Sugar hit after sugar hit. I was eating as much junk as I could, and I was eating it as quickly as I could.

All that fast food was slowing me down. I had never been much of an athlete at school – I was never picked for any teams, and I certainly didn't win any races. Aged nineteen, I couldn't even shuffle a quarter of the way around the local park before my body, swollen and clogged with fat, screamed at me to stop. That was hell on Earth. I had always been big as a child, but this was the heaviest I had ever been. Even at six foot five inches, nineteen stone was massively overweight, with my doctor warning me I was obese. I was already sluggish, with knee pain because of my weight, and, with the way I was eating, I was only going to get heavier. How long before I couldn't even make it a quarter of the way around the park?

I'm not going to say I was broken, but I wasn't happy either. Happy wasn't on the horizon. Happy was just a word on the polystyrene box that the kids' meals came in. I had grown up in Hackney, a part of London where I wasn't expected to do much or to become much. But there was a small, persistent voice in my head wondering whether there was more to life than being shouted at by impatient, rush-hour customers who had trains to catch. 'Where's my burger?'; 'Come on, give me my chips': that was the soundtrack to my life. All around me, people were going places, to work, school, university. While everyone else was getting on with their lives, I felt stuck. I had a feeling that I needed to push on with my life, and to make something of myself, but I hadn't yet discovered what that was or who I wanted to be.

I say it was a moment that changed my life, but actually my epiphany in McDonald's lasted a little longer than that: nine minutes, split into three rounds of three minutes each. It was mid-August, a warm, sun-bleached Sunday, the final day of the 2012 London Olympics, and I was on a break with an hour to kill. The television in the break room, which was tuned to the BBC, happened to be showing a fight – live pictures from Anthony Joshua's gold-medal fight in the super-heavyweight division. Looking back now, it's crazy to think my life turned on when I took a break that day.

If I had walked into that room just a few minutes later, I would have missed the fight. Perhaps I might have later seen a headline in a newspaper, or a short clip online or on the news, but then I wouldn't have experienced the emotions I'd felt during that fight. My adrenaline wouldn't have spiked, and I wouldn't have felt such joy. I now call him AJ, but back then I knew him in name only. It was a close fight which could have gone either way, with AJ coming through lots of adversity to beat the defending champion, an Italian boxer called Roberto Cammarelle. More than anything else I had seen in my life, that fight spoke to me, and it spoke with urgency and clarity.

Taking in every punch, just a few miles from where AJ was fighting, I was mesmerised as this young British boxer achieved his dream. AJ's life changed that day, and mine did too. I can't fully explain how I felt, and how my perspective and ambition suddenly shifted in that moment. 'You can do that,' I told myself. I knew what I wanted to do with my life: I wanted what AJ had: I wanted to box at the Olympics.

While I had been going to a boxing gym on and off for a couple of years, I hadn't taken the sport at all seriously until then. Boxers who are serious about their training don't tend to weigh nineteen stone. There was absolutely no reason why I should have believed in myself. How did I imagine I had it in me to compete at the Olympics? I didn't look like an athlete, or even fully understand what it meant to be an athlete, and yet I immediately had this belief in my abilities to make it as a boxer. It was that belief – as ridiculous as it might have seemed to others at the time – that would allow me to make my own dream a reality.

Watching that fight forced me to make a change. As I walked away from McDonald's that night, I said to myself: 'You know what, I'm going to train full time.' I didn't hang around. The very next day, I told my

I'm here to tell
you that change
is coming in
your own life.
You might not
be able to see
it today, but the
day is coming
when you'll
change your life.

manager that I was quitting to become a boxer. While walking away would mean a financial hit, I was still living at home with my mother, who would support me during those early years. My manager wished me good luck. If he thought I was mad, he was too polite to say. I was a nineteen-stone novice with a new and seemingly impossible dream of making it to the 2016 Rio de Janeiro Olympics.

That was crazy enough. The even crazier part is that I would accomplish what I set out to do, that I ended up qualifying for the 2016 Olympics, despite having no previous international experience. I like to think that's a record; I don't know any other Olympian who has turned their life around that quickly.

AJ always finds it inspirational when I tell this story – that I accomplished so much so quickly. It also blows my own mind how, in a moment, my whole life changed. I occasionally still train in the park where I once couldn't even complete a quarter of a lap. It's just that now I can do seven or eight laps comfortably. And then I remind myself that if I hadn't watched that fight, I would still be feeling lost, not fulfilling my potential.

I'm here to tell you that change is coming in your own life. You might not be able to see it today, but the day is coming when you'll change your life. I want to pass on the message that you can get yourself out of any situation you're in right now and find a way of improving your life. You're going to help yourself, and maybe even your family, in ways that you can't even imagine right now. I hope that my story might inspire you to take that first step. If I can go from obesity to the Olympics in four years, and then become a professional boxer, then what might seem impossible to you right now is worth fighting for.

IN SHORT:

- Anything is possible.

- Change is coming – you might not see it today or tomorrow, but the day is approaching when you can start to change your life.

- Once you know what you want to do, start making changes immediately. Don't hang around.

Find your ambition

There's nothing special about me; I suppose that's my message for you in its simplest form, this entire book distilled into one short sentence. Whichever way you look at it, I'm not exceptional, even if I'm doing exceptional things. I'm not freakishly gifted. I wasn't even sporty at school. I'm also not freakishly ambitious. I certainly wasn't born ambitious, which is some people's explanation for how I transitioned so quickly from minimum-wage, zero-hours-contract burger-flipper to elite boxer.

They seem to think that there's something in me that isn't in most people, that I have a drive and an ambition in my mind that other people simply can't access in theirs. They're wrong about that. I used to be quite lazy before I started boxing; that's why I had a belly.

There's nothing special about me; I suppose that's my message for you in its simplest form.

First I found the ambition inside me – through watching Anthony Joshua win a gold medal at the 2012 London Olympics and having that moment of clarity that I wanted to box at the next Games. Then I chose to work on that ambition, and it grew and grew. Committing to boxing helped me to acquire an ambitious mindset. I was pushing hard and becoming hungrier to achieve great things with my life. Boxing was helping me to get in shape, to burn off my fat. The more time I spent in the gym, the more I could see how my body was changing, how I was losing weight and becoming a fighter, and that's when my ambition grew. From small initial targets, like losing a kilogram, I moved on to bigger and bigger goals, like shedding another ten kilos. If I'm ambitious now, it's because I've chosen to be, not because I was born that way. You have to decide for yourself whether you want to find your ambition.

If you're telling yourself that there's nothing special about you, as if that's a reason for not doing anything with your life, I'm telling you that no one's special. We all have the power within ourselves to push and to do great things. You just have to get that ambition out. You might think that you don't have the ability or the drive to do something with your life, but that's probably because you've never tried before.

We all have the
power within
ourselves to push
and to do great
things.

Once you start working hard, and seeing the results you get from being ambitious, you start to set new ambitions for yourself. Once you're on the roll, you pick up momentum and confidence, and it looks to others as though you've always been the ambitious type. But the truth is that you have to start somewhere. That you have to make the first step to finding that ambition within yourself. Sometimes you just have to stop thinking and talking about something and actually do it.

Once you've started, you'll see the mental barriers falling away. As soon as I watched AJ win gold and I became ambitious, it became the most dominant force in my life. It determines the choices I make, what I eat and how I train, and how I spend my days. I do whatever is necessary to win my next fight and achieve my dreams.

If you haven't yet found your ambition, and what you want to work towards, you should be honest with yourself. Most people know what they like and what they're good at. We know what makes us smile. If there's something that makes you happy, there's a good chance that you can make a career, and a life, from that.

If you're unhappy
and you feel
as though you
want to make
changes in your
life, but you're
just not quite
sure what those
changes are, you
have to keep on
searching for
your ambition
until you find it.

If that doesn't work, I urge you to experiment until you find something that brings the drive and the ambition out of you. If you're unhappy and you feel as though you want to make changes in your life, but you're just not quite sure what those changes are, you have to keep on searching for your ambition until you find it.

Sometimes that means taking a risk.

If you're in a job you don't like, staying in it might stop you from finding a better one that's going to transform your life. All the time you spend in a job you hate, you're making yourself more unhappy, and you're not giving yourself the time and the space to find what you really want to do with your life. Even if you have less money for a short while, it's going to be worth it in the long term if you find your ambition.

When you're ambitious, you're making changes, and aiming for something you don't have, and that's not easy. I find it helps to speak openly about my ambitions. Soon after being inspired by AJ winning gold at the 2012 Olympics, I was telling people that I would represent Great Britain in Rio de Janeiro in 2016. People thought I was some crazy guy from

Hackney, walking around making big claims. But I had said that was what I was going to do and so that's what I set out to accomplish. Similarly, I told people that I would win a world title, so that's what I worked towards. Being so open about your dreams will reinforce what you want to achieve.

If you fall a little short, you know there's going to be someone to remind you that you didn't quite do what you said you would. People are scared of failure and ridicule. But just think about what you did accomplish, and how close you did get. Would you have achieved so much if you hadn't been so ambitious? Don't ever be ashamed of your ambitions, of wanting more for yourself and your family.

IN SHORT:

- Everyone has it in them to have ambition, drive and hunger.

- No one is born ambitious - you have to find your ambition. It's a choice.

- The more you accomplish, the more ambitious you'll become. You'll gain confidence and momentum and want to achieve more.

- If you're still looking for something to work towards, be honest with yourself - keep on searching for your ambition until you find it.

- Focus your mind on your goals by speaking openly about your ambitions. Don't be ashamed of being ambitious and aspiring to do something with your life.

You've got
to keep on
telling yourself:
'I want this.'

Believe in yourself – even when others don't

In the beginning, there's often a fine line between delusion and the self-belief that lets you achieve your dreams. Perhaps I was a bit deluded when I committed to boxing. What did I really know then as an amateur about making it as a professional athlete? But if you're going to change your life, or do anything meaningful, you have to truly believe. You can't do anything half-heartedly.

You've got to keep on telling yourself: 'I want this.' Sometimes you'll know where you want to get to, but you won't know how you're going to get there. If you truly believe, you'll eventually find a way to achieve your dream, even if you're not successful the first time you try. If you have any big doubts, and you don't think you're ever going to get to where you want to be, there's no point even starting out on that journey. You're going to be wasting your time. It's not going to lead anywhere. I was never arrogant, but I always had total belief in myself.

Some people won't understand what you're trying to accomplish. But that's OK. It's not their journey; it's yours. Others might doubt you, question you, and even ridicule you, but all that matters is that you believe in your vision. You have to push on, no matter what other people might say. You're the only person who is living your life. You have to live with the moves you make and the moves you don't make. If you believe in yourself, and have a vision for what you're trying to achieve, you must stay true to that and never lose that belief.

Throughout my career, I've had people telling me that I was on the wrong path, that I was crazy, that I was wasting my time. Even my own mother wasn't on board at the beginning, though eventually she came around to the idea! Others took longer. In the early years, there were always critics reminding me how few people made it in sport. What chance did I have of success?

IN SHORT:

- You have to truly believe if you're going to be successful – even if that means you're a little deluded when you're starting out.

- Others might doubt you, question you, and even ridicule you, but all that matters is that you believe in your vision, and that you stay true to that.

- Keep on telling yourself: 'I want this.'

Engaging with social media is a choice – you can always ignore your critics

Even now, after all I have accomplished, I've still got people trying to bring me down. If I go on to Twitter or Instagram, there are always negative voices telling me that I'm 'shit', that I'm a 'hype job', that I'm nowhere near as talented as my promoter and my publicist might suggest. Others will criticise my style or say that I'm getting knocked out in the next fight.

When I was younger, I attracted lots of criticism and I used to react more. I couldn't help myself and would respond, firing back an angry comment that would inflame the situation. But, with age, I've gained a little wisdom and I think I've found a better way of navigating social media. You have to recognise social media for what it is. It's like going into a room where everyone else has their faces covered and you're saying in a small, pleading voice: 'Do you like me?' Ask yourself why you're dancing for likes and validation. Shouldn't you be getting all the confidence and belief you need offline, from the real world?

If you're going to be successful in whatever you do, the belief and confidence has to come from you, not from strangers who don't know you. And you certainly shouldn't allow strangers on the internet to negatively affect how you feel about yourself and your ambitions. If you're comfortable with yourself, and have a strong sense of who you are and what you're hoping to achieve, it won't matter what others say. People don't do this very often but spend some time thinking about who you are as a person, what matters to you and where you're heading. Once you're calm and confident about yourself, there's nothing that people can say that can affect you. Words can't damage you if you know your truth.

You have to recognise social media for what it is. It's like going into a room where everyone else has their faces covered and you're saying in a small, pleading voice: 'Do you like me?'

You get to choose whether you're on social media and you get to decide what you're going to take from it. If I never wanted to see another tweet or Instagram post again, I wouldn't; I'm choosing to be on there. You too need to make the right choice for you; only use social media on your own terms. If I don't like what I'm reading, I can always delete the apps. Ultimately, it doesn't matter what others think of you and whether they believe in what you're doing. What's important is that you believe in yourself.

Most of the time, I don't read the comments under my tweets and Instagram posts. I mostly ignore the trolls. When I do look, I always keep in mind where the comments are coming from, and remember that trolls are unhappy people. That's why they're trolls in the first place, searching the internet to share some of their misery and negativity around.

As you get older, you realise that hurt people hurt people; they're the bullies and the trolls. It's only people who haven't got anything going on in their own lives that bother seeking out others to attack. To this day, I've never seen anyone who's doing better than me and thought: 'I'm going to criticise them or put them down.' I've never messaged

Ultimately, it doesn't matter what others think of you and whether they believe in what you're doing. What's important is that you believe in yourself.

someone something rude or spiteful, especially when I see they are grinding and trying to get somewhere.

Trolls have a lot to say about subjects they know nothing, or next to nothing, about. In my experience, it helps to look at a troll's account and ask whether you would take advice from that person. Because if you wouldn't take advice from them, why would you take criticism from them? Trolls want a reaction. They're probing and testing you with their comments. Try to ignore them. Don't give them what they want.

It's hard to take trolls seriously when I know that they wouldn't dare say anything critical to my face. They're hiding behind their iPhones and their anonymous social media accounts. They don't actually mean what they say online, and aren't speaking with any knowledge, so why should I bother reacting to it?

IN SHORT:

- Belief should come from within – not from strangers on the internet. Ask yourself why you're dancing for likes.

- Don't inflame the situation by sending an angry reply.

- Why would you take criticism from a troll when you wouldn't take advice from them? Remember that trolls usually know nothing, or next to nothing, about what they're talking about.

Why be ordinary when you can make your own path?

I'm a vegan boxer. I punch people for money but don't eat meat and that makes me a rarity. I'm cool with that. I have people in boxing, including nutritionists, questioning what I'm doing, and I always say to them: 'Look at my record, look how many meat-eaters I'm knocking out.'

I haven't eaten meat since turning professional – that's four years now without steaks or chicken wings – and I feel good about that decision. I eat a lot of beans, mushrooms and lentils and that keeps me ticking over nice and strong. If you find something that works for you – and I feel fitter and leaner since becoming a vegan – it doesn't matter what other people are saying and doing. I don't care that most boxers eat meat. You should always be prepared to do something different. Don't be guided by social norms because then you'll be exactly that: normal. If you just follow the crowd and popular opinion, and you're always influenced by what everyone else is doing, you're not going to do anything amazing. You can't stick with the tried and tested and expect to be extraordinary.

If you find a niche and something that works for you, then go for it. In the beginning, people will say they don't understand why you're choosing to go your own way, and why you want to stand apart from the crowd. But if you have some success, as I have with my boxing, you can be sure that those same people are going to start getting curious about what you've done, and will want to copy you. In my opinion, this is about more than success: doing your own thing also helps you to feel happy, as you're doing what's right for you. Whatever you want to do, just do it, just as long as you're not hurting anyone or doing anything illegal. You're the one living your life, and you'll know what works best for you and will help you to reach your goal.

I care about animals but I'm vegan because it makes me a better boxer. Initially, I did a trial, to see how I felt without meat, and I felt so good that I carried on. I'm punching hard and I feel fitter and lighter than when I was eating meat, though I'm also training differently now to how I did back then so that must also be a factor. You might say I've come a long way since the days when I lived off Big Macs and Haribo sweets. Being a vegan, and being on my own path, gives me an edge against all the meat-eaters.

Rather than running with the pack, I'm always happy to go my own way. In 2020, I recorded my first hip hop tracks and the lyrics aren't what you would expect from the genre. I've always listened to a lot of hip hop and unfortunately a lot of the music that is out there is about gang culture, rapping about selling drugs and carrying knives. I still listen to it because I like the beats, and when the bass is big it helps me to push myself in training. I still know certain people who live that gangster life so the lyrics are relatable to me. It always seemed to me that you had to be a gangster to make the music I like. But then I realised that it didn't have to be that way, that I could make a different sort of hip hop.

Just like most hip hop, I'm still rapping about money and women. But I thought that my music could be an opportunity for people in legitimate jobs to flex. You don't have to rap about selling drugs or stabbings. I'm rapping about winning fights, knocking people out and being on holiday in Dubai. It's not humble. In the lyrics, I'm showing off to motivate people what I've done in a legitimate job. The video I shot also wasn't humble – showing a life of Ferraris, rooftop swimming pools and expensive watches. I hope that's inspiring for some people.

As a teenager, I used to do some rapping on the block but I could never have predicted that I would one day be making music videos in Dubai. Success opens doors and lets you do things that you couldn't imagine were possible before. Once you find your focus and push towards your goals, your hard work will lead to more opportunities. From now on, I'll be listening to my own music before fights. How many other boxers can they say they pump themselves up before fights with their own music?

Once you find
your focus
and push
towards your
goals, your
hard work will
lead to more
opportunities.

IN SHORT:

- If you stick to the social norms, you can only ever expect to be normal. Don't be afraid to be different when it could help you be extraordinary.

- When you do your own thing, rather than following the crowd, you're more likely to feel happy and fulfilled.

- Don't worry if others question what you're doing. Once you have some success, they'll soon be copying you.

Focus on yourself: don't waste energy being jealous of others

Jealousy gets you nowhere. Actually, it's much worse than that: jealousy pulls you back and drags you down. Jealousy means you've allowed yourself to be distracted from the person you should be focusing on: yourself.

When I'm with Anthony Joshua, I don't feel jealous of his mansion, or the cars lined up in his drive, or the millions he has in his bank account. I don't obsess over the things he can buy that I can't. That's also true when I'm with another wealthy friend, Umar Kamani, the billionaire founder of fashion brand Pretty Little Things. I'm not interested in all the shiny objects around them, and how big their homes are. Instead, I'm fascinated by what motivates them, in the conversations they're having, and in what they're doing every day to stay at the top of those fast-moving and unforgiving industries. What keeps them focused, driven and successful? That's what I care about. And I care because I want to know how I can apply those lessons to my own life.

Maybe you're suffering from jealousy. Let me tell you that if you just stop looking at someone with envious eyes, you'll soon start learning how they've become successful.

If you're living a truly blessed life, I want to be around that. I'm not going to be jealous of you, but I'm going to learn from you. Umar is one of the most inspirational people I know. When he calls or messages me, I always learn something.

If you're busy thinking about other people's wealth, you're going to be wasting time and energy that you could be using to push your own life forward. You have to take responsibility for your own life.

You get to
determine the
rest of your
life. It's really
that simple:
you decide
where your life
is heading.

Boxing is one-on-one – that's a reminder that it's up to me whether I succeed or fail. One of the reasons I love boxing is that it's all down to me. I'm not reliant on others. Win, lose or draw, it's on me. That helps with dieting, and going for an extra run or doing a few more sit-ups. When all is said and done, I know that it's going to be me against that other guy. I know that he's going to be training just as hard. When it's time to knuckle down, I'm motivated by how it's down to me. I'm focusing on myself and what I'm capable of.

But that principle also applies to everyone's life. You get to determine the rest of your life. It's really that simple: you decide where your life is heading. One of the best ways of propelling yourself through life is to stop looking around you with jealousy and envy, and to start trying to learn from successful people.

I've learned so much from AJ over the years. After everything he has accomplished, he's still grinding. He's dealing calmly with hyper, crazy situations. If he has any setbacks, he's bouncing back. That's what I'm looking at, at the core of who he is as a man, rather than all the shiny things on the outside.

There was one time when I looked at AJ and felt jealousy. It was a few months after I watched him win his gold medal at the 2012 London Olympics. I was out in London and just happened to see him outside a nightclub. I asked him to pose for a picture and told him that I was also a boxer, though I didn't say how he had inspired me. The reason for my jealousy was that AJ got into that club and I didn't.

Our next meeting was in a gym, after my coach arranged for me to spar with him. I was still a fan then, rather than a friend or a fellow professional. He was a big, strong, dangerous guy, while I was still an amateur and it was an intimidating moment. But I managed to hold up pretty well and he said to me afterwards: 'You're mad tricky. You're good.' From then on, I would travel to his gym in Essex whenever he wanted to spar with me.

I heard that others were scared of sparring AJ, but I wanted to learn from him. AJ came to respect my ambition, my hard work, my graft. It was surreal when he started following me on social media, but not as crazy as when he asked me to go to a party with him. That's when I thought to myself: 'Wow, are we actually friends?' It didn't seem real that someone I had looked up to for so long was saying to me: 'Hey, bro, let's go out to a party together.'

AJ has done so much to help me. I think about the position that I was in when I watched him win the gold medal, and I think about what I've achieved since then, after being inspired by him. How could I possibly feel jealousy or envy? If I had focused on what he had that I didn't, how much energy would I have wasted not getting myself where I wanted to be? Don't be intimidated by others' success; learn from them, and make them your allies.

If you're always comparing yourself to others, you're not going to make yourself happy. I feel as though everyone gets what they deserve. If I'm upset about the money that someone else is making, I'm not going to be thinking about my own blessings. Think about what you have in your life, and the blessings you have, rather than obsessing over what others have. If you want what they have, find your ambition and work for it.

Your perspective will dictate your level of happiness. We're all blessed in our own way. When you're focused on other people's blessings you're forgetting about your own. I'm trying to be the

If you're always comparing yourself to others, you're not going to make yourself happy.

best possible version of myself. I'm not measuring myself against others because that will only make me miserable.

IN SHORT:

- Instead of being jealous, try to learn what made that person successful, and how you can apply that to your own life.

- You're responsible for your own success and happiness - you get to determine how the rest of your life goes.

- Comparing yourself to others is only going to make you unhappy - we're all blessed in different ways.

Stand up for yourself

Above all the sound and the fury on my street corner that day, I could still hear the quiet, persistent voice in my head, the one that was telling me: 'I'm going to die today.'

If you haven't lived in my world, you might think that the word 'gangsters' conveys a certain glamour. Even I once glamourised gangsters. Well, let me take some of the glamour out of London's gangsters for you. Encircled by twenty of these gangsters, some of whom were on edge – high on testosterone, adrenaline, menace and whatever else – and spitting out their threats to 'shank' me, I was only surrounded by ugliness. The situation wasn't looking good for me. I was just fourteen years old, a child. Getting stabbed was a very real possibility. Another possibility, and this was hardly much better, was being jumped on – getting kicked, punched and trampled in a terrible blur of feet and fists.

While I was never a gangster myself, I knew gang members and I also knew what they were capable of. Growing up in Hackney in the 1990s and 2000s, you would constantly hear about the stabbings, the blood on the streets. This wasn't playground talk, the tall stories that most children like to tell each other: I had seen some of that gang violence with my own eyes. I didn't have to imagine how these situations sometimes ended. In my part of London, stabbings were just a part of childhood, something you got accustomed to hearing and seeing, but it feels very different when, for the first time, it looks as though you're about to become a victim.

This was different to street fights; I had been in plenty of those. I was genuinely scared for my life. 'We're going to shank you up, we're going to stab you up,' some of the circle were saying. This situation was playing out on my road, just metres from my front door. Now I wasn't just concerned whether I would live or die, but also how much my mother might see.

'What have I done this time?' I asked myself. The answer, of course, was that I hadn't done enough to deserve being in this situation. This had been provoked by a playground fight with one of the younger gang members. He had made fun of me for being fat, pulling up my T-shirt to expose my belly, and I had given him a black eye. Someone in the gang had found out where I lived. That boy I had fought was now front and centre, and the other gangsters were telling me how this would go: 'He's going to hit you in the face as many times as he feels like right now and you're just going to let that happen. If you touch him just one time, we're going to finish you off.' Voices around me reminded me that some of the gang wanted to stab me; they were talking as if standing there, taking the punches without defending myself, was a good option. Maybe it was. That was the option I was taking.

My little brother was there, as a witness to this. But I didn't want him involved. Essentially, I was on my own. There were twenty of them and just one of me. Even if I let the boy hit me, what was stopping them from all rushing me? I couldn't predict how this would end. I knew that I could beat this boy up; I just didn't want to. I didn't even want to throw a single punch.

Boom. The boy hit me with his first punch, which connected with the side of my head. I didn't punch back. Boom. He hit me a second time.

For now, this was a punishment beating and I was used to those. I had been bullied since primary school, from the age of eight or nine. I was a fat kid with a funny name, Ikechukwu, which was my first name when I was in school – I drew a lot of attention to myself. Britain wasn't a kind place if you were different. Kids weren't taught about other people's cultures. Even the teachers couldn't pronounce my name properly.

The beatings could be savage. The bullies would make me stand still in the street, and I would let them take as many free shots as they wished. Punches to the head. Punches to the body. If a group of them rushed me and I dropped to the floor, they would get their kicks in. Everyone would get their thrills.

There were always more of them, and they were always older. It got worse in secondary school when my bullies went through puberty and had their growth spurts. While I was big for my age, I was still a child, and physically they were already young men. I would feel empty, beaten down, defenceless. If I fought back it would make it worse; they made that clear.

That would make them angry and the beating would continue for longer.

The only thing that would make it stop was when they felt as though they had made me suffer enough on that day – when they were bored of beating me. It depended on their mood on the day: how many punches would satisfy them? But, the next day, they would feel the urge again and they would hurt me again. I took a lot of damage over the years.

Maybe they thought I could take the beatings because of my size. Often it was the local gangsters who were picking on me. There's another word you can use for gangsters: bullies.

Other times, the bullies made me fight in the street after school. They would approach me in the school corridor and tell me that I was fighting after lessons were over. I didn't have a choice. I was like their dog in a fight. I didn't have a problem with the other boy. Often, I had never even seen him around before. But I was expected to punch the other boy, and he was going to hit me back. If I didn't do what they said, they would hurt me. You don't have to tell me how mean kids can be. The bullying happened in and out of school. Once they used a girl I liked to lure me towards the back of the playground. I realised too late it was a trap, and they bundled me into a shed, locked me in and left me for hours. I would have ended up sleeping there overnight if a teacher hadn't heard me calling out.

Standing up for myself had never felt like it was an option for me. I felt as though getting physically bullied was something I just had to deal with. But something had changed around the time that the twenty gangsters confronted me on my road.

I remember standing in front of the mirror, giving myself a pep talk that it was time to change. This had a lot to do with self-worth or self-esteem. For years, I hadn't valued myself enough. It was as if I somehow deserved to get picked on and roughed up by gangs of bullies. Perhaps it had been a gradual process, building up to that moment, but that was when I articulated how I felt. I told myself that I would no longer accept this, that I was better than this. I realised that I valued myself too highly to allow others to treat me like that. That wasn't just about dealing with bullies; it was about every occasion when someone thought they could walk all over me. I was no longer going to allow that.

Looking back, there was something cinematic about the moment that I decided I was going to stand up for myself, that I was no longer going to allow that boy to use me as a punchbag. I was going to fight back. I knew the risks involved. I knew that if I hit him, they could all rush me. But I also knew that if I let the boy swing at me, the other gangsters would probably still jump me anyway. Whatever I did, I was almost certainly going to get hurt. What I was no longer prepared to do was stand there and take it. I was going to fight back, even if that meant getting stabbed.

The first twenty gangsters had come by bike and on foot. Now more were arriving by car. Did they have dogs too? The situation was escalating. I hit the gangster once and he dropped to the floor. His head was on the pavement and I was thinking: 'This is really it. I can't undo what I just did.' I could sense some of the gang members were edging forward, saying that they wanted to attack me and get this over with. Fortunately, a few other voices said the two of us should continue fighting. The boy was back on his feet saying he wanted to resolve this one-on-one. Now I was moving, avoiding his punches. Then I hit him again and he was back on the floor. I had busted his nose. There was so much blood spraying everywhere that several of his boys removed their tops to soak it up. 'Stop, stop, stop,' the boy pleaded.

In that moment, with that one punch, I changed how people saw me. I also changed how I saw myself. 'You can properly fight,' the boy said, still holding a T-shirt to his face. That was a signal to the rest of the gang that this was resolved, that he didn't want them to step in and finish me off. From fearing for my life just moments before, I was relieved to hear one of the gangsters say: 'No one is going to touch you now.'

That was a mad afternoon when I hit someone so hard that the gang wanted to be friends. This might seem crazy to you, after what had just happened, or what had almost happened, but I even ended up chilling in the park with them the rest of the day. They had a new respect for me and I was relieved this was the end of it. I remember it as the day that I learned to stand up for myself. Word got around. I was no longer the guy who stood there and took the pain. I was the guy who fought back, even when there were twenty gangsters around me. From then on, I was no longer a target in the area. The bullies and the gangsters melted away. That was the power of standing up for yourself. I was lucky that day. Some of the gangsters there that day

More often than not, if you stand up for yourself – verbally, or physically if necessary – people will have a new respect for you. Even better, you'll have a new respect for yourself.

ended up in jail for violent crime. When they said that they wanted to stab me, that wasn't an empty threat. They had meant it.

I hope that you'll never find yourself in a situation as dangerous as the one I just described. The point of the story wasn't to teach you about punching local gangsters, or necessarily about dealing with violence. I just hope that it illustrates the importance of standing up for yourself, and having the self-respect to stop a situation from continuing. More often than not, if you stand up for yourself – verbally, or physically if necessary – people will have a new respect for you. Even better, you'll have a new respect for yourself.

IN SHORT:

- Don't let people walk all over you – don't ever think that you deserve to be bullied or tormented.

- Giving yourself a pep talk can give you the courage to stand up for yourself.

- When you stand up for yourself, it changes how others see you and also how you see yourself.

Don't be a victim of your past

I'll be going about my day in London and then I'll suddenly run into one of my former bullies. I haven't moved far from Hackney, and they're mostly still in the area too. I had a lot of bullies as a kid, and I see them around.

I haven't forgotten what they did to me. The beatings when I couldn't punch back. The times they rushed me, hitting and kicking me to get their thrills. The afternoons they made me fight against other kids after school. The daily, relentless savagery of it all. But there's no animosity or anger on my part. I've forgiven them for what they did and moved on with my life. I'm happy with my life, but can't tell you how they feel about theirs.

Those encounters must be much more awkward for them than they are for me. They'll remember what they did to me, just as I'll recall what went on, but they don't bring that up in conversation. They don't say sorry and I'm not expecting them to either. It all goes unspoken. Bringing up the bullying is about the last thing they're going to do. Back when we were at school, they couldn't have possibly imagined that the guy they were getting free shots at would become a boxer.

My former bullies are in their late twenties and early thirties now. Some of them have their own kids. We're all grown up now. I'm not going to dwell on what happened when we were kids ourselves. They tell me it's great to see me and how proud they are of what I've accomplished as a boxer, and they might ask me to pose for a picture. A few of them have even said that their younger siblings look up to me, that I'm a role model and inspiration for their little brothers. It's crazy how these things go.

I'm very happy to speak about my past, but I won't let it define me. I talk about that time in my life because it helped shape me as a person. If you are being bullied now, I want you to know that you'll get through it and that all will be OK in the end.

I'm not a victim. I won't let myself be defined by what happened years ago. My whole life wasn't determined by what went on in the playground and outside the school gates. I've achieved so much in my life since school, and rate myself highly as a boxer; why, then, would I see myself as a victim of my past?

Some people have gone through some horrible stuff and I don't want to be insensitive or minimise that. But I've also met many people who have experienced some relatively minor drama and they've decided that they're going to be a victim forever. They'll tell you they would have done something special in their lives if it wasn't for that. Or they'll excuse certain behaviour patterns because of some event in the past, and they think it's OK to continue acting like that. They don't realise that being a victim is damaging their chances of ever achieving great things.

Being a victim is easy. People cling on to that victim status and hide behind it for the rest of their lives. It's hard to properly address certain events in your past. It's hard to get over stuff. It takes thought and energy and really opening yourself up. That's why people choose to hide behind the past. That gives them a

You mustn't allow something in the past to hold you back. You have to unlearn that and push past it.

reason for not pushing to be successful. You've got an excuse for failure.

You mustn't allow something in the past to hold you back. You have to unlearn that and push past it. You need to be tackling your problems and your past rather than making excuses for the rest of your life, though of course I understand that some people will find it harder than me to overcome trauma. If that's you, you shouldn't be hard on yourself, but you will hopefully find that the next chapter, on therapy with pen and paper, might help you to deal with your past.

You need to hold yourself in higher regard. You're allowing yourself to fail because it's easier that way. But that's such a negative way to live your life. If you think like that, you're going to lose too many dreams.

IN SHORT:

- If you choose to see yourself as a victim, you'll lose out on your dreams.

- If you allow yourself to be defined by your past, you're allowing yourself to fail.

- Change how you see the past - instead of breaking you, what you've been through has probably helped you to become the person you are today.

Therapy with pen and paper: write down your problems

Even for a boxer with fast fists, there's sometimes nothing more powerful than a pen and paper. When I'm going through a hard time, or feeling low, I've learned that one way to deal with my problems is to write them down. Often the best and the quickest therapy is scribbling my concerns on a piece of paper.

I'll talk about the power of friendship later in the book – I'm always willing to share my problems with my friends – but I also find that it helps to write them down. You might already be comfortable with talking openly with your friends. Perhaps you're not. Either way, I can recommend putting pen to paper. Or, if you prefer, writing a note to yourself on your phone or laptop. Whether on paper or a screen, it's a private way of being completely honest with yourself, and fully addressing your problem, because you can be sure it's not going to go away until you've dealt with it.

Every time I'm finding something challenging, or I'm angry or sad, I'll write down what's going on and how I'm feeling. Perhaps I feel as though I've let myself down in my training session, or I'm having girl problems. I'll break it down into three parts: what happened; why I think it happened; and how I might stop it from happening again in the future. My problems always look smaller on paper than in my head.

Sometimes, I work something out in my head while I'm writing it down or creating a mind map of my thoughts: it just suddenly clicks for me. Other times, I'll go back to the piece of paper before having that moment of clarity when I see the path forward. Having it there on the page, in black and white, always helps, whether immediately or a little later down the line. It's also useful for me to look back at past problems and to think: 'Remember how you felt when you

My problems
always look
smaller on
paper than in
my head.

wrote this.' That's a reminder that you go through good times and bad times, in your professional and personal lives, and you can survive the dark moments.

Occasionally, I'll pin my notes and pieces of paper on the wall in my home, or inside the gym at my training camp, to remind me of how I've dealt with past problems. There are old pieces of paper floating around in my house; the other day I found one inside my Great Britain kit bag, which was like discovering a time capsule of my feelings and emotions as an Olympian. Once I've corrected a problem, I like to push on to the next thing, but it's always good to refresh your mind so you don't repeat old mistakes again in the future, and you can also appreciate how far you've come.

I've been writing notes to myself for years, ever since I lost an amateur fight in 2014 and hated how I felt. I picked up my pen and started writing because I wanted to be sure I was doing everything to avoid feeling like that again.

Just before the qualification tournament for the Olympics, I took a loss, and for the first time I briefly questioned whether I was good enough. I fretted about my lack of international experience. I made a plan of action, writing down all the little things I could do to improve, such as fitness, technique, sleep patterns. I broke that down into everything I could do each day to make it happen. It was bits and bobs, like telling myself to go for a run every day, and that really helped me. I came back with a vengeance in that tournament and won it.

The main thing is that you're honest with yourself because, if you're not, this isn't going to help you find a way forward.

In my experience, it also helps to write down more positive emotions. When you're feeling low, you want to remind yourself of the good times.

IN SHORT:

- Face your problems down and reach for a pen and paper – otherwise they are going to come back again and again.

- Write down what happened, why you think it happened, and what you can do to stop it happening again.

- Pin your writing on the wall to remind yourself of how you dealt with past problems.

- Also write down positive emotions, which you can reread to help you through the dark times.

Don't let impatience kill your dreams

Most celebrities want you to think they were an overnight success. They'll post on Instagram about how quickly they went from being a nobody to a big deal. In almost all cases, that's not a true story. It's so far from the truth it's not even the airbrushed truth. They don't want you to see how hard they have been grinding and grafting – they would prefer you to think they got there on talent alone.

I would love it if more celebrities could be honest with people and show all the energy, sacrifice and emotion that has gone into them being successful. They should be happy to say they've been working for years because there's no shame in that.

People today are more impatient than ever. This celebrity culture is damaging because it creates the impression that overnight success is most people's experience, that you usually don't have to be patient and persevere. I understand people don't want to work for years. They want to go directly to being successful, skipping out the tough part in-between. But that's not how the world works.

I'm happy to tell you that I wasn't an overnight success. I think it's important that you know that about me. Perhaps you imagine I had overnight success because I had that moment in McDonald's watching Anthony Joshua winning gold and I immediately knew that I wanted to be an Olympian too. But knowing what you want to do with your life is one thing. Going and doing it takes years of graft. While I've achieved my dreams faster than anyone could have possibly imagined, and I've been working at record speed, my success has still been years and years in the making. You can go viral in an instant, but anything more meaningful is going to take a while longer.

When you're changing your life you need to be bold but you also need to be patient. The greatest mistake you can make is not trusting the process. If

When you're changing your life you need to be bold but you also need to be patient.

you're trying to lose weight, looking for a new job or attempting to make any other significant change in your life, you'll want something to happen right here right now. That's natural; we all crave a quick fix. But the danger is that when you don't get immediate results you'll give up. That's the biggest hurdle that many people have to overcome before changing their lives. You have to tell yourself that you're building the foundations, and that you're going to have success in the future, just so long as you stick with it.

If you're impatient and you abandon your dreams, the whole world might miss out on something special. If you're telling yourself, 'It's not working out. I'm going to scrap it', you're not giving yourself a chance. A lot of brilliant ideas have probably been lost because people have been too impatient.

I'm forever reminding myself of the importance of being patient. Early on in camp, I won't be in peak condition with my fitness, strength and endurance. Because I've been in great shape before, and I've been able to do great stuff in the past, and now I'm not able to do it as well, it's frustrating. In those situations, I tell myself: 'Relax. It's going to come.'

Sometimes your goal seems so far away but, if you believe in it, you have to stick with it.

As a boxer, there's lots of repetition when you're training for a fight. You're doing the same stuff again and again. You're lifting weights. You're going for runs. It's the same feeling over and over again of being tired. When it all feels samey, that's when you need to be patient. Whatever you're doing, you're going to have to repeatedly practise, graft and hone your skills, and that can be monotonous.

Others are going to drop out and give up at that moment but you're different; that's when you make your dreams a reality by being patient. On pages 82-87, I've written about how targets and measurable goals can help make work a bit more fun, but alongside those numbers you're going to need the mental resolve to get where you want to be. Keep on going; it's going to be worth it. Your future self is going to thank you for what you're doing right now.

The reality is that you won't be an overnight success – you're likely to have years of grafting ahead – but your success will be all the sweeter for that.

IN SHORT:

- Don't expect to be an overnight success because hardly anyone is. You should expect to work hard to achieve great things.

- Others might give up on their dreams because they don't have immediate results but that's when you're going to show your patience.

- Your future self is going to thank you for the work you're doing now – your success is going to feel even better when you finally get there.

PART 2
YOU'RE GOING TO NEED A PLAN

Now that you've figured out how you want to transform your life, you need to start thinking about how you're going to create that change. You can't rely on luck – you can be sure you won't get far without a strategy and without having measurable goals to work towards that stop you from lying to yourself. In this second part, I'm also going to be passing on my insights into turning fear to your advantage, and the importance of getting uncomfortable and taking some risks. You should be questioning everything, learning from your failures and asking others to hold you to account. While most people don't like talking openly about money, I'm very happy to, and there's a chapter on how you should think about wealth.

Don't believe in luck – always have a plan

The way some people talk about me, you would think I'm the luckiest boxer in the world. That I've only got to where I am today because of some outrageous good fortune.

For years, I've had people telling me I'm lucky. It started when I was an amateur. Apparently, I was only on the Olympic team because I got lucky. Then, when I turned professional, I was accused of being lucky again. People said I was only working with Anthony Joshua's management company and with Eddie Hearn's promotion company, Matchroom, because Lady Luck was a fan of mine.

The reality, of course, is that no one comes into Hackney and just offers to sign you up and make a life for you because they're in a generous mood that day. It doesn't work like that. There are hundreds, if not thousands, of boxers who are all pushing themselves and looking for opportunities. You need the raw ability in the first place, but after that you need the ambition and the strong work ethic. I've had people telling me that I'm lucky that I can punch so hard, which makes it sound as though I've done no training, and that the power in my fists is all down to good genes. There are people who are even better physical specimens than me, but they can't fight or punch hard because they haven't trained for it.

When someone calls you lucky, it devalues all the hard work and sacrifice that have gone into you achieving your dreams. It's as if you've played no part in your own success, as if you're somehow just a bystander to your own story.

I used to find it extremely frustrating and annoying when I was called lucky, but now it no longer bothers me so much, probably because I have a better understanding of why some people like to say that about others.

When someone
calls you lucky,
it devalues all
the hard work
and sacrifice
that have
gone into you
achieving your
dreams.

Dare to Change Your Life

I've achieved a lot in a short space of time, which is why everyone seems to think that I've been blessed with good luck. I can see how it would be easy to become obsessed with the idea of luck when others around you are having success and you're not. You start to think that you've been cursed with bad luck and that everyone else has had good luck. But if that's how you see the world, in terms of good luck and bad luck, you're not taking enough personal responsibility for your own life. If you're the person who is putting someone else's success down to luck, it's probably because you don't want to look within yourself and face the fact you haven't worked as hard.

People will say anyone could have achieved great success if only they had had some fortune along the way, but I don't believe that's true. You don't get to where you are because of luck, but because of the work you've done. People talk about lucky breaks - but I believe in being ready for any opportunities that might come your way, and that's down to all the hard work you've done over time. If you're not completely ready to take that opportunity it's going to pass you by. That's not bad luck, that's a lack of preparation, and an opportunity missed. If you work hard, you're going to put yourself in situations where things happen for you.

IN SHORT:

- If you're always thinking and talking about luck – saying that others are lucky, and that you're unlucky – you're not taking enough personal responsibility.

- If you're calling others lucky, you need to look within yourself and face up to the fact you haven't worked hard enough.

- You should be ready for any opportunities that might come along.

Measurable goals mean you can't lie to yourself

The absolute worst part about being a boxer is 'making weight'. Most boxers would say the same. I adore the fighting, even the training, but there's nothing to love about getting my weight down to two hundred pounds.

That round number is the upper limit for cruiserweight, the highest division after heavyweight, and the one I fight at. You might think that two hundred pounds sounds like a lot - that's fourteen and a quarter stone, or just over ninety kilograms - but consider that I'm naturally much heavier than that. I'm a big guy. I'm six foot five inches, which is tall for someone in my weight division, and between fights I weigh more than two hundred pounds. If I'm going to fight, I need to be at or below that number at the weigh-in, which takes place around thirty-six hours before I step in the ring. One pound above that number, though, and I won't be fighting for a belt.

Two hundred. I think about that number for weeks, months even. It's not always front and centre in my mind, but it's always there somewhere. As the fight gets closer, that number moves to the forefront.

Making weight can be hard sometimes, but I've hit the target every time during my career so I know I can transform my body again. But I want to be bang on two hundred. I don't want to go too low because then I won't be in peak condition for the fight. To help me make that target, I'll weigh myself regularly. A few months out from the fight, that means weighing myself a couple of times a week. During that stage of my preparations, I'm focusing on my fitness and strength, while also trying to get my weight down. In the last few weeks before the fight, I'll become even more meticulous about losing weight and will step on the scales every day.

Weighing myself becomes part of my daily routine. Looking at my weight each morning allows me to track my progress and to understand what I need to do.

Whatever you're trying to accomplish in your life, you need numbers that allow you to track your progress. This is the era of data – you should be able to find a way, maybe even an app, of quantifying the progress you're making. All targets need to be measurable. Numbers put everything in black and white. Numbers mean you can't lie to yourself. If you have a target that's measurable, you'll know when you're on track, when you're exceeding it, and when you have to work a little harder to catch up. If I wasn't weighing myself every day, I would just be looking in the mirror and assessing how I look. I would be telling myself that I seem fit and that I've been dieting. But I need to get on the scales to understand what's going on.

Knowing that I have to make weight adds pressure when I'm going out and when I'm eating. Every bit of enjoyment I get from my food, and from eating the occasional bad meal, also comes with the knowledge that I'm going to have to work it off. 'Enjoy yourself right now,' I say to myself, 'but the future Lawrence is going to have to deal with this pizza.' If I wasn't

Whatever you're trying to accomplish in your life, you need numbers that allow you to track your progress.

measuring myself regularly, it would be easier to let things slide a little, and then I wouldn't be on track for the weigh-in. Numbers give me discipline.

From the beginning, I've always associated boxing with weight loss. That was the reason I walked into a boxing gym in the first place in 2010 – to burn off the belly. Back then, I had targets for the weight I wanted to lose, and meeting those targets pushed me to set some more. While preparing for a fight, I do more than just stand on the scales. For a more detailed analysis of my body, I'll have a scan that tells me how much fat and muscle I have, and also what my bone density is. I get numbers, such as fat percentages, for every part of my body, and can compare those figures to previous scans so I can see how my body is changing.

Numbers also help me to push harder in the gym, which is why I use a heart-rate monitor and look at other data, too. Am I throwing more punches than I did last week? How much more weight am I lifting than in the last session? And did I run faster and further today than yesterday? When you're doing the same exercises again and again, having those measurable goals helps to make my training more exciting and interesting. Ultimately, those numbers help me to push myself.

Once I've made weight, I have thirty-six hours before the fight to enjoy food again. I'll be significantly heavier by the time I walk into the ring. Having been so careful for weeks, I'll suddenly be eating larger portions again and that's probably a shock for my body. But I love that part of my preparations when I'm giving my body the calories it needs for the fight. Eating all that pasta and pizza also gives me endorphins, and that means I'll be feeling happy when it's time to fight.

As a boxer, you'll always have a number to aim for. You should also give yourself a target: it'll stop you from lying to yourself about the progress you're making.

IN SHORT:

- Numbers put everything in black and white – they mean you can't lie to yourself. Numbers give you discipline.

- Whatever you're doing with your life, find a way of measuring your progress regularly.

- Having a target will make your work more exciting and interesting and will help you to push yourself.

You need
a strategy

As a boxer, you know that if you ever get into a bloodbath, when both you and your opponent are taking damage and the ring starts to look like a crime scene, people are going to love you for it.

But I'll never willingly splash around in a bloodbath. I've seen the fighters who've been in bloodbaths and they're the ones who end up in hospital beds and who are now struggling to speak.

The art of boxing is to hit and not get hit. It's not allowing your opponent to hit you because you think you're going to hit them more. Boxers who get into bloodbaths are only doing it because they're limited fighters and it's the only option they've got. They're often more concerned with entertaining the crowd, and putting on a show, than with winning, and that mindset comes from a lack of ability. They want to be the tough guy and for the crowd to love them. But no one should willingly take punches to the head. It's all about strategy.

You might know what you want in your own life, but do you know how you're going to get it? I've got ambitions and I know how I'm going to achieve those goals. While I occasionally have a few impulsive moments in other parts of my life, I think through everything I do in the ring. There's a strategy, as there should be in your life in the pursuit of your own dreams. It was Mike Tyson who said that everyone has a plan until they get punched in the face. You always need a strategy to prepare you for that very moment – always be prepared.

Plan A is always to box clever, to hit and don't get hit. Don't let opponents get any work off. Grind them down. As a professional boxer, I'm fighting over twelve rounds. It's more about strategy and endurance and knowing that you can't go all out all the time, but you have to pick your moments when you make your moves. You train differently for professional fights, with longer sessions, and the strategy also needs to be different.

Whatever you're doing in life, you want to be proactive rather than reactive. Try to be the one who sets the rhythm. I'm extremely awkward in the ring. That's just the way my body is. I'm tall and I can't dance. But my opponent is going to be dancing to my awkward, natural rhythm.

If you stick to your strategy, eventually you'll grind your opponents or rivals down – have confidence in your plan. I'm breaking my opponent down, both mentally and physically. I know that if I'm winning every round, and they're getting frustrated, something happens to them. I see it every time. There'll be a moment when they succumb and tell themselves: 'You know what, I'm going to lose today, there's no point resisting for much longer.' I can feel that moment because immediately the fight gets much easier. Everyone fights hard in the first three or four rounds, throwing their hardest punches and moving well, but after a while you realise that their punches are getting slower. They're looking at the referee to intervene, to break us or perhaps even to tell them the fight's over. They start falling to the floor because they're getting weaker. I'll give them a nudge and they'll go flying across the ring.

Whatever you're doing in life, you want to be proactive rather than reactive. Try to be the one who sets the rhythm.

I can't remember a fight when I wasn't in control. I've been dominant throughout. Until someone forces me to bring something else out, I'm going to dominate the way I know. If I'm getting outmanoeuvred or out-worked or out-classed I'll go to Plan B, which is to be the big strong guy who brings the pain, with more exchanges, but that obviously comes with more risk. But no one has forced me into that position yet. I've got Plans B to E, but no one has seen them yet.

Stay strong and stick to your strategy. I'm not going to let loose now, and try something other than Plan A, just because that might entertain the crowd. I don't feel that pressure. I'm doing whatever I can to win my fights. I feel as though I'm cruising through my fights. I haven't had a fight yet where I've shown why Anthony Joshua, Tyson Fury and Dillian Whyte have all had me in their training camps and why they've all touted me as a top fighter. No one has brought that out of me yet and also I don't feel the need to bring that out unnecessarily. All that matters is that I carry on winning. People don't always remember how a fight was won but they always remember the winner.

It can help to break your strategy down into small chunks of time. I might have a mini-strategy for the next ten seconds, and then another mini-strategy for the ten seconds after that. The entire time I'm in the ring, I'm thinking about strategies and how I'm going to win the fight.

It's the very opposite of going looking for a bloodbath.

IN SHORT:

- Knowing what you want is just the start – you also need to have a strategy for how you're going to achieve your ambitions.

- Don't feel as though you need to impress anyone – only do what's going to help you accomplish your goals, and don't try to put on a show.

- Be proactive rather than reactive – you want people to be dancing to your rhythm.

- Stay strong and stick to your strategy.

- Break your strategy down into small chunks.

If you truly
want to change
your life, and
push yourself
to new heights,
you're going
to have to take
some risks.

Get uncomfortable: you need to take some risks

Playing it safe gets you nowhere in life. At best, you'll stay where you are today. More likely, you'll drift backwards as others will rush past you. If you truly want to change your life, and push yourself to new heights, you're going to have to take some risks.

Ultimately, if you don't take any risks, you can't expect to enjoy different results and new, bigger rewards. If you only stick to what you know and what you've done before, you might also end up regretting why you limited your chances. If you always feel comfortable with what you're doing, you're not taking enough risks. I wouldn't be in the position I am today, just four years after turning pro, if I hadn't been a risk-taker. Taking risks is part of being a champion and a winner. You don't become a champion by forever seeking comfort.

Some people told me I was taking things too fast. They didn't want me to take certain fights as they felt they were too risky at that stage of my career. They would say to me that I didn't need to fight the guy straight away, and that it could be pushed back, but I would always reply: 'No, I want this now.'

Some boxers like to talk up big fights for years and years, but I've always pushed for fights to happen sooner rather than later. I don't want to spend years waiting for a risky fight when I could have it straight away. I'll tell myself that if I can't beat this guy, then all my dreams are built on nothing, and I would rather know that sooner rather than later. I want to see what I'm made of and what my level is.

I'm just going to keep pushing and pushing. I've fought undefeated boxers, fighters who had more experience than me, boxers who had been through wars. They all thought they had the power to knock me out. They went to bed the night before thinking they were going to win, and they had thousands of people who believed the same.

But I didn't believe the same. And I went out there and proved myself.

If I hadn't taken the riskier fights, and had played it safe throughout my career, I wouldn't have made anything like the progress that I have done.

I'm not suggesting that I take wild risks with my career or that you should in your life. I'm talking about calculated risks. I'm not saying a young boxer should take on Mike Tyson in his first fight. You have to be smart. I knew that some of the fights I had were going to be tough, but I was always confident that I would win them.

I can see what's happened with other boxers who haven't embraced risk like I have. They're really talented fighters, but they're not where they could be. They don't want risky fights as they're scared of losing and having to rebuild their careers. They won't get future opportunities. Some people just want an easier life. I understand that. But if you take it easy, and don't embrace risk, you'll never discover what you're capable of.

You're capable of more than you realise. We can all push ourselves beyond what we thought our limits were. Going beyond my limits in training – by lifting heavier weights than ever before or setting a new personal best for a run – is more exciting for me than my actual fights. I expect myself to win my fights, but I can shock myself in the gym or on a run by realising that I can do more than I thought. I love those moments when I'm pushing myself harder than ever before.

Whatever you're doing, you can push yourself more than you think. I'm always excited by what I'm achieving in the gym because I wasn't naturally athletic as a kid and teenager. I've had to build all this. Some people live for the training. I don't. What I love is the feeling of pride from beating my record and pushing myself to new extremes. Being fit isn't my natural state. My natural state is eating food. I've reached fitness levels that I could never have imagined, and yet I still keep pushing myself to new heights.

When I'm preparing for a fight, I like to train by gradually building up, so each week I'll be lifting heavier and heavier weights, and running that little bit faster. I won't rush myself in the first days of fight camp, as I don't want to tire myself out or get injured, but I'll build and build until I'm in peak condition and that's when I shock myself sometimes. When I'm in peak condition, I'm pushing to get beyond my limit. And if I can't get there today, I'm going to try tomorrow.

People are scared of leaving their comfort zones. That's why they don't try to push themselves. They're scared of what it might look and feel like. From my own experience, I can tell you that you can touch that limit and tell yourself you're doing OK and you can go further, even if it's just a little bit. Then, the next day, you can push it a bit more. Your body and mind will find a way to survive.

IN SHORT:

- If you want some changes in your life, you can't play it safe – you need to take some risks.

- If you don't take risks, you'll never find out what you're capable of.

- You shouldn't take wild risks – they should be calculated risks.

- You're capable of more than you realise so keep pushing.

- There's nothing more exciting than pushing yourself to new extremes.

- Don't be scared of what it's going to look and feel like when you push past your limits. Your body and mind will find a way to survive.

Don't waste energy on things that are out of your control

The world was coming to an end. There was no more professional boxing, no more dreams of a world title, but that was just the start of my problems. I was preparing to drink the rainwater that was collecting in my garden. I imagined that the power grid was going to fail and that London, along with every other city in the world, was about to go dark.

In truth, I had probably watched too much *Black Mirror* and other dystopian series on Netflix, which was why I thought that the coronavirus pandemic would bring about the collapse of modern society. Lockdown had just started, we couldn't leave our homes, and I thought that even the water supply was about to dry up. If it came to it, I could survive at home drinking rainwater. I was also ready for a world without electricity: I was going to play lots of chess and other board games with my housemates as the world collapsed around us.

Thankfully, I never actually drank any rainwater as the taps kept flowing. But the pandemic did stop me from fighting for much of 2020. In the end, I didn't fight for over a year, from late 2019 to December 2020, which was by far the longest gap of my professional career. Until the pandemic hit, I had been in the rhythm of fighting every three months or so, and then suddenly I had such a long break, with my fight for a world title postponed, pushed back and then rescheduled again (and in the end I fought, but not for the world title, as my original opponent tested positive for Covid). That wasn't ideal, as having a date for your fight, and knowing that you're working towards a big moment, is what gives you focus and discipline as a boxer.

You have to
be able to
tell yourself
that there are
certain things
you can control
and other things
you can't.

During lockdown, I was still training and keeping things ticking over, but I wasn't able to get together with my trainer or my strength and conditioning coach because of the strict social distancing rules that were in place then. There was also the financial uncertainty (see pages 135–40 for more about money).

The pandemic was an extreme example of why it's important to have the tools to be able to cope when things are out of your control. You have to be able to tell yourself that there are certain things you can control and other things you can't. As I reminded myself, you can only do your best and focus on the things you can do something about. The stuff I can't control, I just let it be. I just need to carry on doing what I'm doing, and to believe that my hard work is going to be rewarded. If you control what you can control, you'll create opportunities for yourself.

When I was younger, I found it harder to cope with the idea that some things were out of my hands, and I wasted energy thinking about that, but with age and experience I've adapted my thinking. Even when I didn't know when I would be fighting again, I still managed to stay motivated and to keep working hard.

When we were all locked down in our homes, it was helpful to know that I wasn't the only one going through it, that we were all in this together. It would have been very self-obsessed of me to have only been thinking about myself, and my frustrations about my fight being postponed, when people were dying or losing their jobs. Thinking about others who were going through much worse than me helped me to rationalise what was happening to me.

IN SHORT:

- Understand that you can't control everything – so concentrate on what you can control.

- If you stay motivated and do your best, you'll be rewarded in the end.

Positive energy goes a long way

Everyone responds better to positive energy than to negativity, and to being around optimists rather than pessimists. In boxing and in life, having a sunny outlook goes a long way. I would like to think I'm an upbeat person. I'm happy with who I am and what I'm doing with my life and that allows me to have a positive energy.

Negativity and pessimism simply aren't part of my make-up. I've never liked negativity, and thinking and speaking badly of myself and of others, as I don't want to have a negative impact on myself and people around me. Even after negative experiences, or spending time with downbeat people, I don't allow myself to be negative. If you feel yourself giving in to negative thoughts, you need to tell yourself that staying positive allows you to achieve more and also helps you to bring people with you on your journey who can help you.

Have a think about how you might come across to other people, and whether they view you as positive or not. Consider the language you use and how you express yourself. Don't waste your time gossiping about others. Have a can-do attitude. You'll know yourself that it's great to be around someone who is excited about what the future brings, and not someone who is gloomy about life.

To help me to stay upbeat and confident I like to surround myself with positive people. I don't want my trainer telling me that my opponent is going all out in training and that I need to work harder otherwise I'm going to be knocked out. I would rather have someone encouraging me and telling me I can do something. I don't think I'm that unusual in preferring that positive reinforcement. I've had trainers in the past who have taken that more negative approach and it didn't work with me.

The first time I met my current trainer, Shane McGuigan, I was struck by his positivity. He's madly

Don't waste
your time
gossiping
about others.

confident. I told him what I wanted to do, including winning a world title, and he said: 'Yep, let's do it.' In that moment, most people would have said: 'OK, mate, take your time.' Right from the start, he said he believed in me. He's as confident about me as I am. That's a big plus. He's also assured of himself and his abilities. He's got his own ambitions about his boxers doing well. Shane keeps a tally of all his wins and losses as a trainer, and I've never seen that before, though it backs up my belief in the importance of keeping track of your progress, which I wrote about in an earlier chapter. When he puts me into certain potentially difficult fights, I know he's confident I can win because that would also be his victory. He gets to put that result on his win and loss sheet. When he says to me: 'You're going to smash this guy', I believe him.

There's more to Shane than positivity, of course. He's a great trainer with lots of experience. When I was looking for a new trainer, I happened to watch an interview he did, in which he made a few comments about me that were totally in line with how I saw myself. He was talking about my awkward boxing style and how I set up certain punches and combinations. Most people don't see that. His breakdown was scarily accurate. I knew then that I wouldn't want him in an opponent's corner. I know what I'm thinking when I'm doing certain things in the ring. He explained to me what I was doing and what I was thinking and I said to myself: 'Oh my god, that's exactly what's going on'. We had a trial and we gelled well.

But, for all Shane's expertise and experience, if he wasn't such a positive person it wouldn't have worked. Our relationship would have broken down very quickly.

Changing your life is easier when you surround yourself with positive people. I've made sure that everyone in my team has an upbeat, can-do attitude. Duncan Ogilvie is my strength and conditioning coach. Out of everyone in my team, he's been with me the longest. We've worked together throughout my professional career. He's an important member of the team. He cares and he shows it. He goes above and beyond being a strength and conditioning coach and takes time out of his day if he thinks he can do something to help me. Will Harvey, my day-to-day manager, who makes sure everything runs smoothly, is also positive. I only want to work with people who bring good energy. Look at the people around you and ask yourself whether they are bringing positive or negative energy into your life.

Changing your
life is easier
when you
surround
yourself with
positive people.

IN SHORT:

- If you have a positive energy, you'll achieve more and also bring people with you on your journey who can help you.

- Think about the language you use, and don't waste your time with negativity and gossiping about others.

- Don't be gloomy about life – have a can-do attitude.

- Surround yourself with positive people who will help you have an upbeat mindset.

Turn fear into a positive force

I feel almost invincible in a boxing ring. I don't fear defeat. I'm not even afraid of injury or death. People get hurt. I've seen how other boxers have suffered life-changing injuries, and some have even died, but I tell myself it won't happen to me. I'm not sure how other boxers think but I expel that idea from my head. I simply won't allow that thought inside my brain. Getting hurt's an impossibility. There's no way that's happening.

That's not to say I don't feel any fear as a boxer. The time for feeling fear is when I'm training. I'll be thinking about my opponent and whether he's good enough to beat me. Often during my career, I've fought boxers who were previously undefeated. They had already been champions. I respected their abilities and was fearful I could lose if I wasn't completely on my game.

I like being the champion, and calling myself undefeated. I'm scared of losing that status. But that flickering fear helps me during training, because without it I wouldn't train quite as hard or run quite as far. I use that fear every day. I'm fearful when I'm a long way from the ring and when no one's watching me. When no one's watching, I'll be training at full intensity. When no one's watching, I'll hit the bags. I do what I need to do so when it comes to fight day, I'll be ready with no reason to feel fear.

Fear will stop you from being slack or sloppy with your preparations. That fear will ensure you invest in your preparations – whether that's time or money – and then when it's time to perform, you'll be as ready as you can be. A few days before a fight, my fear fades away.

Of course, there are nerves, as I've done all that work and now it's time to perform, but nerves aren't the

Fear will stop you from being slack or sloppy with your preparations. That fear will ensure you invest in your preparations – whether that's time or money – and then when it's time to perform, you'll be as ready as you can be.

same as fear. Once the fight starts, I use the nerves to my advantage to power me through. You shouldn't see nerves as negative: nerves allow you to focus your mind on what really matters, on your purpose and strategy. Nerves are something positive. They show you're excited, that you care.

Whatever you're doing, try to use fear as a positive force in your life. It can be the fuel that makes you work harder than ever before. When you're preparing, feel scared that you're not going to achieve your dreams. But when the day comes, you mustn't allow fear to cloud your judgement as you can't think clearly when you're afraid. If you've done enough preparation, you don't need to be afraid.

Fear stems from the unknown. You don't know what's on the other side. You don't know what's coming next. And that terrifies you.

That's why fear melts away with experience. The more you do something – whether that's boxing, performing in public or anything else – the less you'll feel fearful. It can be useful to understand that when you're starting out. I certainly wished I had known that when I had my first amateur fight, when my heart was pumping so fast in my chest, and I was in fight-or-flight mode and operating purely on instinct. Though I won that fight, I couldn't remember a thing. The whole fight was a blur; there wasn't a single moment, even one punch, that I could recall. I wasn't focused on what I was doing.

That's what fear does to you. It scrambles your mind so you can't think straight. You're relying on instinct and you're reactive, always responding to your opponent's move. If you can control your fear, and use it to your advantage, you can think and act strategically. In any industry, you won't get very far if you can't put your plan into operation.

If you're scared of something, expose yourself to that fear. You'll probably soon realise you had nothing to be genuinely fearful of.

IN SHORT:

- Fear can be a positive force in your life. Fear will make you work harder to achieve your ambitions.

- Fear melts away with experience – the more you do something, the less fearful you'll feel about doing it again in the future.

Don't let fear put you in dangerous situations

As a young man on London's streets, or in other cities that have a knife crime problem, you might find yourself carrying a weapon, or moving with people who are carrying something. You're thinking you only have two choices: you can either be the aggressor who does the damage, or you can be the one who's looking at the other end of that blade. Both of those choices come from fear. Some of my friends' decisions, born out of fear, cost them their lives or their freedom.

I didn't realise it at the time but when you're in that environment, when you won't leave the house without a weapon, your entire life is governed by fear. That knife in your pocket changes everything. When you're carrying a knife, you're going to end up in situations you otherwise wouldn't do, and you're going to act differently because you have that weapon to hand. When you're acting out of fear, you don't make rational decisions, and that always ends up costing you.

As I got older, I started to see the world a little clearer and thought to myself, 'Hang on a minute, I can control this. I just won't go to some places and put myself in certain situations, and there will be less of a need to move with certain people or to carry weapons.' When you're no longer carrying a knife, you react differently. It's a different situation. Once I became a lot more self-aware, and a lot less scared, I made better decisions.

People often ask me what it feels like to punch someone. The truthful answer is that I don't feel anything at all. I don't do this out of anger or fear so I don't get relief from delivering the punch. The only time I'll feel anything is when I land the punch that wins the fight – then I'll be happy and relieved. If I get punched, I don't let it break my focus. I know that if I stay focused, and stick to my strategy, I'll win the fight.

You can apply this strategy to your life: prepare so you don't fear the unknown; and think things through so you don't put yourself in dangerous situations that force you to feel fear and stop you from having a clear head. When the punches come, stay focused on your goals.

IN SHORT:

- Fear can put you in dangerous situations. Take a moment to think about the choices you're making.

- Prepare so you don't fear the unknown – that will help you to keep a clear head.

You can apply this strategy to your life: prepare so you don't fear the unknown; and think things through so you don't put yourself in dangerous situations that force you to feel fear and stop you from having a clear head.

Learn from failure: question everything

No one likes losing, and defeat can make you question everything. Get knocked down and even when you're back to your feet, and your headache clears, it still feels as though your world is rocking.

Defeat feels like a bigger disaster for a boxer than it would be for any other sportsman or woman. That's because every boxer knows the value of staying undefeated. Talk to any promoter, or potential sponsor, and they'll tell you that it's easy to sell that word 'undefeated'. As a boxer, you're not competing as often as other athletes, and you're building your career and your profile, and you're trying to protect the zero in your loss column.

Everyone loves a winner, and you know that a first defeat is going to take some of the shine off your status. Especially if you're still on the way up, and still making a name for yourself, it's going to be more challenging to come back from that. When you face failure, most likely you're going to be asking yourself the same questions and trying to work out what your future looks like.

In boxing and in life, your approach to failure can determine whether you're ultimately a success or not. Are you going to fall apart and lose all confidence? Or are you going to take the opportunity to learn why it went wrong?

I experienced defeat as an amateur. I'll always remember how I felt after losing just before the qualification tournament for the 2016 Rio de Janeiro Olympics. I remember because the lessons I took from that defeat are still with me; that amateur defeat helped to turn me into the professional boxer I am today.

If a defeat makes you question everything, as it did for me, that's no bad thing. Questioning everything

You often don't have to make dramatic changes to recover from a failure – the difference between success and failure might be very small, with just little tweaks required.

allows you to examine every aspect of your life and make changes that will allow you to become a better fighter in the future. Doing a full review of my life – which for me included even looking at when I should be drinking caffeine and when I should be going to bed – allowed me to reset and rebuild. And I've kept that same energy, of examining everything I do to be the best I can possibly be.

You often don't have to make dramatic changes to recover from a failure – the difference between success and failure might be very small, with just little tweaks required.

I'm always happy to talk and think about that defeat because it brings back the emotions that I felt that day. The sting of defeat can propel you to greater things in the future. For a boxer, defeat brings mental and physical pain, and the mental pain can often be worst when you feel as though you lost the fight rather than the other guy winning it. If you can tap into that feeling again, you can use that to push yourself harder in the future. The memory of that defeat is still one of my main motivating factors in training today.

IN SHORT:

- Failure can make you question everything in your life – make the most of that opportunity to learn how to do better next time.

- Your attitude to failure can determine whether the experience makes or breaks you.

- Don't forget how you felt when you failed, and use that emotion to work harder.

Get real: review your priorities

You need to get real with yourself. As often as you can, you should review what you're doing. Look in the mirror. Examine all aspects of your life, and ask yourself whether you're doing everything in your powers to achieve your dreams. No one knows better than you what's going on in your life. Be completely honest with yourself: have you got your priorities right?

I had to get real with myself when I was preparing for my fight in December 2020, which would have been for the world title if my original opponent hadn't tested positive for Covid just days before. That was a huge opportunity but, with just twelve weeks to go,

I didn't feel as though I was acting as though it was – not a hundred per cent anyway.

I was on it with my training, but I was still seeing people, still having a good time, and still going to bed late. 'Is this how you expect a world champion to be training? Is this how you expect a world champion to be behaving?' Those were the questions I kept asking myself and as the answer was no I knew I had to change things rapidly.

After getting real with myself, I turned it on and went all out with my preparations for that fight. No one could have trained harder, or dieted better, or focused more. If a girl wanted to come to see me at midnight, as fun as it might have been, I had to say no as I had training in the morning. If a friend wanted to come over and make some music, they got the same response: I would tell them that I needed to be completely focused on my preparations.

I'm constantly reviewing my priorities. Earlier in my preparations for that fight, during the first lockdown, there was a moment when it hit me that I didn't have my priorities right. That moment came when I opened my wardrobe. Hanging there were all the reminders of how much I had spent on designer clothes, and what a waste of money it all was now there was nowhere to go. I just thought: 'Wow.' I had all these expensive jackets and trainers, but I didn't need any of them.

Growing up, I had been obsessed with designer clothes, along with jewellery and cars. Now I had them, who was it for?

No one really cares what you're wearing, as long as you look alright. My friends didn't care – they asked me about my plans for growth as a person, not the labels I was wearing. They'd seen me in ten different pairs of trainers, and told me that I could have invested that money instead. Or bought some new training equipment. 'I guess designer clothes are more important than your job,' they would say.

I listened, of course, and took in what they were saying, but it was looking at my wardrobe during lockdown that it became perfectly clear to me how I had got this so wrong. With everything shuttered in London, including gyms, I realised something else that was as shocking as my collection of designer clothes: I had no training equipment at home. I didn't even have a bag to hit. With all the money that I had spent on clothes and shoes I no longer liked, I could have bought myself a bag, some weights and a treadmill.

I didn't have my priorities right; I had put more money into looking good in clubs than into preparing myself for my fights.

IN SHORT:

- Every so often, ask yourself whether you're doing everything you can to make your dream a reality.

- You've got to be real with yourself – be completely honest.

- If your priorities aren't right, you need to make rapid changes.

Ask others to hold you to account

Before one fight, I told my housemates they could fine me £100 if they ever caught me with chocolates or a bag of Haribo sweets. For weeks on end, I was living with the cola bottle cops. The threat of having to pay a fine, and with it the acknowledgement that I hadn't stuck to my diet, stopped me from giving in to the temptation of Haribo Mix.

I hold myself accountable when I'm getting ready for a fight, and I'm self-motivated to get up and do the training. I don't need anyone to drag me out of bed in the morning. But I also ask those around me to hold me to account at all times. You shouldn't be afraid of asking your friends for help to make sure you're sticking to the path you need to be on (and in turn you should be willing to help them). When I know that my friends are always watching to make sure I'm doing everything I should be, that could be the one or two per cent difference in my preparations that ensures I'm in peak condition on fight day.

I'm always inviting my friends, and those I work with, to judge me by the highest standards, and I suggest you do the same. Give them permission to scrutinise everything you're doing. You can't hide what you're doing – you have to keep on pushing and grafting because they can see exactly what you're up to.

To help me before my fight in December 2020, my friends had the idea of buying some whiteboards to put up around the house. One board was on the fridge telling me not to eat this and that, and not to snack after a certain time, and the other one had motivational quotes.

My friends are looking out for me in the virtual world as well as in the real world. I don't want to be wasting my money on designer clothes, and so if I post a picture on Instagram and my friend thinks I'm wearing a new top he'll message me. There's no escape from my friends and that's exactly how I want it.

Asking others
to hold you to
account also
makes your
friends feel as
though they're
on your journey
with you.

Asking others to hold you to account also makes your friends feel as though they're on your journey with you. If I'm hitting the bag in my home gym, and they're around, I want my friends to be in there cheering, and making sure that I'm doing it with full intensity.

Winning belts isn't just a victory for me; it's a group win. We're all part of this, everyone who's connected to me.

IN SHORT:

- You need to be self-motivated but asking others to hold you to account can help you to stay disciplined.

- Let your friends fine you if they catch you doing something you shouldn't be.

- Asking your friends to hold you to account will make you feel as though they're on your journey with you.

Money – let it motivate you to help others

I used to look up to drug dealers and gangsters. They were the ones with the money and the cars. Growing up in Hackney, in London, it was the gangsters who had the chains and the nice clothes, and the pretty girls sitting by them.

Maybe a few others from Hackney had done well - from football or singing, perhaps - but they had long since left the area after they 'blew up'. But the gangsters still came to the block to say hi. The people we saw doing well and who were still there, the ones we could talk to every day, were the gangsters. As a young kid, that makes an impression on you.

This isn't an attack on the hood – I still know people who live that life – but I've shown that you can have an exciting lifestyle with a legitimate job. You don't have to sell drugs to have that life. If you work hard enough, you can even live a bigger life than the drug dealers. And I can enjoy my money without any concerns. I'm not worried that the police are going to knock on my door and take my car and my jewellery. There's a paper trail of how I made my money. I can spend my money as I please without thinking that the police might be watching.

Some people aren't honest about money. They care about it much more than they'll ever let on. I'm happy to be honest about money. I'm comfortable saying that money is a massive motivation for me. I don't come from money. We didn't have much when I was growing up. My parents didn't have a house or any assets. We lived in a flat and I shared a room with my brother. When I was younger, that was all I knew. All my friends in primary school, all the other kids on the road, lived in flats too. But then, as I got older, and saw others living in houses with big gardens, the world opened up to me. I realised that the world had more to offer. Naturally, you start to want more.

You can have an exciting lifestyle with a legitimate job.

Just before my first fight as a professional, in 2017, I had just £7 in my bank account. I now live in a house with a back garden, with a gym at the end of the garden, and that's a blessing to me. When I was a young kid, I couldn't have even fathomed living in a house like this.

Boxing has given me the ability to set my family up for life. Belts and accolades are great, but they aren't going to put food on the table or pay for the renovations to my mum's house or help my family in other ways. If I had a choice between a world title fight for free and another fight for money, I'm always going to choose to get paid. I know what that money can do for those around me.

As much as I want to live a certain way – and I like cars, holidays and watches – my financial priority is to give back to my family. I want to be a good son, a good brother and a good father in the future to my kids. I want my parents to feel comfortable in this life, and I want to be able to pass on money and assets to my kids. It's more of a motivation when you want money for others rather than for yourself. Once I feel as though everyone around me is sorted, I'll be able to enjoy myself and spend more on the things that I like.

KNOW YOUR WORTH

Whatever industry you're in, you need to make sure
that you're getting your fair share, that you're getting
paid what you deserve. I do a very dangerous job.
I need to be compensated for that. People around
boxers are making money – the television companies,
the promoters – so the fighters need to get our share.
We're the guys in the ring. Boxing wouldn't exist without
us and the contracts need to reflect that. Most likely
your job won't be as risky as mine, but do your research
and ask around in your industry to discover whether
you're being paid enough. If you feel as though you're
underpaid, don't be too embarrassed to ask for a raise,
using that research to explain why you deserve more.

SPEND IT WISELY

Use an app on your phone to keep a close control
over what you're spending, and whether you're
earning enough to maintain the lifestyle you want.
With all the delays and uncertainty caused by the
coronavirus pandemic, I wasn't paid for a fight for
over a year. I thought I was going to be rich and then
suddenly I was having to adapt my spending and look
after the pennies a little more.

During lockdown, I got better at saving money, though there were still bills to pay for my coaching and strength and conditioning training. But I see that as investing in my career and helping me to make more money in the future. Everything needs a plan. Make sure you have yours clear in your mind.

IN SHORT:

- Don't be embarrassed to say that money is a massive motivation for you. It is for most people so you might as well be honest about wanting more.

- Earning money to help others is more of a motivation than spending it on yourself.

- Make sure you're getting paid your fair share, and don't be embarrassed to ask for a raise.

- Keep an eye on your spending so you know what's coming in and going out of your account every month.

PART 3
KEEP
HUSTLING

If you're going to make big, lasting change in your life, you can't ever stop hustling. In this third part, I'm going to be sharing my lessons on how to keep on working towards your goal, including exploring the power of practice, and why projecting fake confidence is a waste of your time. To stay motivated and focused, you should surround yourself with people you trust, you must always be curious, and you'll have to make some sacrifices. Among other lessons, I'll also look at the importance of sleep, and why you shouldn't be afraid to open up and show some vulnerability, even crying in front of your friends.

The power of practice

How do you prepare for the punches that are going to come your way in life? Like anything, it takes practice.

For me and my career, that's why sparring, or practice, is probably the most important thing I do before a fight. As the fight camp continues and the sparring becomes more intense, I feel my eyes improving and I become better at reacting to the onslaught. I get sharper. That helps me to be comfortable in the ring on the day of the fight. Sparring allows me to become accustomed to what I have to do on fight day, in a more controlled environment. When it comes to the fight, I'll be used to the fire, the pressure, the hustle and the physicality of being in the ring.

The preparation for every fight is different but ideally I would want six weeks of sparring, of which four weeks would be hard sparring. I'll do up to twelve rounds of sparring in a session. Sometimes I'm asking my sparring partners to go all out in a session as I want a physical workout, but on other occasions I'm lowering the intensity slightly as I'm working on something technical – it's more of a learning session. Before I start practice, I'm always clear what I'm trying to get out of it, and I think that applies to anyone – know what you're hoping to improve today.

Out of everything I do to prepare for a fight, sparring gives me the most satisfaction as it's the closest I get during camp to an actual fight, and it gives me a strong sense of what I'm working towards. With all the gym work and running, I'll know that I'm fit enough for the fight, but when I'm sparring I can feel it all coming together. Sparring does amazing things for fighters.

If you're going to succeed at anything, you have to practise, and you have to practise how you want to perform. That means bringing the same level of intensity and focus to your preparations that you're going to want when you're performing. If you're not used to operating at a high level you can't suddenly

Know what you're hoping to improve today.

expect to make that jump when you're doing it for real. I would also suggest trying to replicate the conditions in which you're going to be performing. For instance, if you're preparing for a presentation at work, could you sneak into the room beforehand and practise in that empty space? And if you're studying for an exam, sit at a desk rather than slouching on the sofa.

Practice gives me confidence going into fights as I've seen myself in training. I've seen what I'm capable of. I know that I've performed well in sparring so when I get in the ring for the fight it's not nerve-wracking. I tell myself that I do this every day, that I'm ready for the onslaught.

Whatever you're hoping to accomplish, you need to practise, and to practice at high levels of intensity, to give yourself the best chance of success.

IN SHORT:

- Be clear what you're hoping to get out of today's practice – you need to be focused.

- Practise with the same level of intensity that you'll be performing at.

- Practice gives you the confidence to perform at your best – you can tell yourself that you've done this so many times before.

Don't bother faking confidence – build real confidence

Before they start throwing punches, boxers are always getting into staring contests. You'll see them at the weigh-in, when they're up close and face-to-face with their opponent for a pre-fight publicity shot, their noses almost touching, and they're both doing everything they can to out-stare their opponent. They daren't look away as they believe that's a sign of weakness and that it would show their opponent, and everyone else watching, that they're scared.

They keep on eyeballing and eyeballing, fighting hard against the blink that they can feel coming.

I'm the complete opposite to most boxers. At the weigh-in, I'm always the first to look away.

As soon as the photographer has got their picture, I'll immediately stop looking at my opponent. I'm not interested in staring contests, or in trying to project supposedly strong body language, such as walking into the ring in a certain way. The reason I don't try to out-stare my opponent is that it's nonsense; it has no impact on the physical fight we're going to have the very next day. The same is true of puffing out my chest as I walk to the ring because it's meant to demonstrate confidence and strength in those final moments before a fight. As I don't feel any fear in those moments, I also don't feel the need to put on a show or to try to prove myself to anybody else. I won't even stare down my opponent in the ring, as many boxers do.

People waste a lot of time thinking about their body language when they should be working on how they really feel on the inside and then their body language will reflect that. Why bother puffing out your chest when you're feeling scared on the inside? You're

People waste
a lot of time
thinking about
their body
language when
they should
be working
on how they
really feel on
the inside and
then their body
language will
reflect that.

going to be wasting a lot of energy trying to maintain an appearance that's fake when you could be using that energy to create real confidence on the inside.

As a boxer, when the bell rings and the fight starts, no one cares whether you out-stared your opponent and how you walked into the ring. Success is based on real confidence in your preparation and skills, and what you really feel inside. What's true in boxing is also true of life – you need to believe in what you're saying and what you're doing.

I wrote in an earlier chapter how, after first daring to change your life, you must believe in yourself even when others don't. If you truly believe in what you're trying to do, and then you go out and do it and you have some success, you can use those moments to build your confidence. Don't waste any of those successes – keep reminding yourself of what you've achieved and how you're capable of so much more in the future. Your confidence will only grow.

Don't bother with all the other stuff that doesn't matter, such as winning a staring contest (or whatever the equivalent is in your world). It might feel important in the moment, and it might add to the show, but in time you realise that no one cares about the fake confidence you're trying to project. It's not fooling anyone and you're only wasting energy that could be better spent on being truly confident. You can be whoever you want to be, and you will find your real confidence, as long as you're hardworking and dedicated.

IN SHORT:

- Don't waste time and energy trying to project fake confidence when you could be working on building real confidence.

- It's important that you truly believe in what you're saying and doing.

- Fake confidence won't help you when it actually comes to doing something.

Open up and show your vulnerability

You tell someone you're a boxer and they think you're a barbarian. But I'm happy to open up and show my vulnerability. I'll discuss all my problems with my friends. I'm comfortable crying in front of them. Life isn't always sunshine and roses and I'm not ashamed or embarrassed to tell you I've had some dark moments during my career and also been through some hard times in my personal life: break-ups, money problems and family rows.

As a man, especially when you're in a world as macho as boxing, it's tempting to pretend to yourself and to others that you're OK. You don't want to admit that anything is wrong because you see that as a weakness or a failing, as if going through a hard time somehow makes you less of a man. Most men don't want to open up and talk about their problems. But I believe that if you don't speak openly about your issues, they will stick with you and bring you down. The best way of confronting your problems, and to avoid repeating them again and again, is to speak openly about them. You need to face them down.

As a boxer, I face my fears and my opponents in the ring and, as a man, I take on my problems by sharing them with my close circle of friends.

Showing vulnerability doesn't reveal weakness. Actually, it's the opposite. It's a sign of strength. You need to have a certain level of confidence to show vulnerability. You're opening yourself up for potential criticism, even ridicule and laughter, and to the possibility of your friends saying: 'Mate, it's really not that big a deal.' There's nothing I won't discuss with my closest, oldest friends, with the guys I've known forever. We go very deep. Nothing's off limits. They know everything about me, and vice versa. They have seen me at my highest and lowest moments. As I live with a couple of them, it would be impossible for me to hide anything from them, even if I wanted to.

Showing
vulnerability
doesn't reveal
weakness.
Actually, it's
the opposite.
It's a sign of
strength.

I've added new friends over time, but I've still got that core group. My old friends are so important to me that we have a name for ourselves, The Penny Bois, and I wear that on my kit when I fight. We try to be there for each other and to help each other through any trials and crises. There have recently been a few media campaigns to encourage men to speak openly about their mental health, and that has helped us as a group to become even more proactive about making sure everyone is OK. When we ask each other, 'How are you?', we're not just saying that as a superficial, empty form of greeting; we really want to know. We're actually listening to the replies and ensuring that no one is suffering in silence.

I'm open with my partners when I'm in a relationship too. My exes have known exactly how I felt. They've known everything about me. I've always been happy to share because that's what makes me stronger.

If you hold everything in and don't talk openly, you'll make situations bigger in your own head than they are in reality. Often, you're in certain situations because you can't figure a way out. Talking about your problems allows you to get a fresh perspective. Your friends might not see the situation as being as big as you had made it out to be in your own mind. They might offer a solution or help you to rationalise what's going on. If you're closed off, and you're keeping everything to yourself, you're denying yourself the chance to have that help and reassurance.

Perhaps you won't want to hear the advice you're getting. But often when you react that way, and don't like what your friends are suggesting, you later come to realise they were right to say what they did. You'll then feel happy that you disclosed your problem to your friends as now you've been given a way out.

You might be reading this thinking that your group of friends is different to mine, that you and your circle aren't as open. I would urge you to start a culture of sharing problems. If you're open with others, that will encourage them to share back. The next time you have a problem, it will be even easier to speak openly. You'll have more open dialogue and people will understand you a lot better. You'll also have a better understanding of others and what they're going through.

I can assure you it's always going to be beneficial to make yourself vulnerable in the short term and to enjoy the long-term benefits of being open. If you hold your problems in, you might feel better about yourself in the short term, as you're kidding yourself that everything is OK, but your problems will get worse in the long term.

IN SHORT:

- Opening up and showing vulnerability doesn't reveal weakness – it shows strength.

- If you don't share your problems, they will become bigger in your head than they are in reality.

- Once you start sharing problems with your friends, they will become more open with you.

Be careful how you share

One reason that boxers don't want to open up about their problems on social media or in interviews is they think it could give their opponents an edge.

When I'm in camp before a fight, I'll always research my opponent online, and I'm sure he is doing the same with me. I'm pretty diligent. I'm not just looking at videos of their previous fights, and clips from their training sessions, but also checking through their Instagram and Twitter. I want to know everything about them: what music they like, what their motivations are, anything that reveals their true personality or character. If I see something that makes them sound weak, I feel as though that gives me a slight mental advantage. If my opponent looks and sounds sad or scared in any of his posts, I'll take some confidence from that.

You, like me, have to be careful about what you put out into the world as it could be turned against you. But that doesn't mean being closed off with your friends, too. And if they betray your trust? Well, they aren't friends you need in your life.

IN SHORT:

- Don't be closed off with your friends, but be careful what you put out into the world as it could be turned against you.

Surround yourself with people you trust

Before I was a boxer, I couldn't get a girlfriend, and I was always the one making the first move and going over to talk to girls in clubs. Now I have a lot of female attention.

While I enjoy the attention, if I'm going to go all-in with a girl, and have a serious relationship with her, I have to be sure she's with me for the right reasons and she genuinely likes me. I ask myself whether she's actually interested in me or if she wants to tell her friends she's dating a boxer.

Whatever your situation, there's a possibility that someone's with you for the wrong reasons. I think

I've got better over time at working out what someone's intentions are, as eventually people reveal themselves in what they say and do. But I've also learned that I shouldn't over-analyse people and that I can't live my life without trust. It's not healthy to immediately distrust everyone I meet, even the girls who make the first move. Having a girl, someone I could trust, would make life a lot simpler. I know from experience that relationships come with their own complications, but it's also complicated seeing a few girls at the same time.

I can sense when new people in my life are hoping to use me to get something. I'll distance myself from them. Training for a fight is the best possible excuse for shutting them out – I can always say I can't meet as I need to be in the gym early in the morning. I'm not looking for new friends. I have my close circle of old friends that I've known forever, so I don't feel as though I need to add to that network. I have total trust in my old friends, and they can also trust me completely.

I'm generally a trusting person. Trusting those around you, in both your personal and professional lives, is crucial if you're going to achieve your dreams. If you can't trust those around you, you're going to be paranoid and on edge, and it's going to hold you back. You need to be able to talk freely, and discuss what's going on, if you're going to have the best chance of success.

I have total trust, for instance, in my promoter Eddie Hearn. That's because Eddie always does exactly what he says he's going to do. As an athlete you're basing your life on promises and contracts, and Eddie always delivers. He always fulfils his promises and creates opportunities for me. He's very clear on the numbers, and the minimum amount I'm going to be paid for a fight. And he always pays me early and in full. Eddie is a businessman and he wants to be the biggest promoter in the world, with the best fighters and the most world champions. He's ambitious and he saw the potential in me to help him with his goals. I know I need to keep on winning my fights, but Eddie has been true to his word.

In the same way, I have total trust in my manager Anthony Joshua and the rest of the team. The sort of business relationship I like is when it's long-lasting and reliable and trustworthy. When you can freely share information that you wouldn't want others to know, information that could be embarrassing or dangerous if it got out. I know that if I want to have trustworthy people around me, I need to come across as someone they can trust, so I try to ensure that everyone thinks they can put their faith in me. That means being true to my word, and showing people that they can share information with me. I'm always looking to build trust in the people around me as I think that helps everything to run more smoothly. Trust works both ways.

IN SHORT:

- You need to trust those around you if you're going to achieve your dreams.

- Don't be naïve, but also don't immediately distrust everyone you meet – that's not a healthy way to live your life.

- If you can't trust the people around you, you're going to be paranoid and on edge and you won't be able to talk freely.

- If you want to surround yourself with trustworthy people, you need to be trustworthy yourself, so always be true to your word.

Keep it simple to reduce the pressure

I'm the Marie Kondo of boxing. You might have heard of Kondo, the Japanese tidying expert who declutters Tokyo apartments; that's me with my mind. In the days leading up to a fight, I'm stripping everything back, keeping everything simple to keep myself feeling calm.

Stripping back for me means tuning out everything that surrounds my fight – such as how shiny the belt is, and how much money I'm going to get paid – and only focusing my mind on what I have to do to beat my opponent. Just before a fight, I'm only filling my brain with the practicalities of how to win. I want to be thinking about my fight in the simplest possible terms.

People often complicate things and build them up in their mind. What you need to do is to shut out everything else and focus on the task in hand.

There's always pressure on me when I have a fight, and it's not going to help me if I'm thinking about how the night could change my life. Cut through the white noise, the hype and the fantasy, I tell myself. It's just a boxing match. I just have to beat one man. Yes, it's on a big stage and there's a TV audience of millions, and there's a belt at stake, but we would be having the same fight if no one was watching.

People often complicate things and build them up in their mind. What you need to do is to shut out everything else and focus on the task in hand. I can assure you that will help massively with your efforts to reduce the pressure you're feeling. All I'm thinking about in training is being in the best possible shape and the strategy I'll need to beat my opponent. In the moments before a fight, all I'm thinking about is my game-plan.

If you're struggling to deal with pressure in your own life, I can recommend doing the same: stripping it back to the basics. Think about what needs to be done rather than what's on the line and what you could gain or lose. Don't let your mind fast-forward to a future of what-ifs.

If you're faced with a big event, to stay composed, try telling yourself that it's just another step on a journey.

Think about what needs to be done rather than what's on the line and what you could gain or lose. Don't let your mind fast-forward to a future of what-ifs.

I know that winning a belt does amazing things for my life, but it's not the start or the end of my journey.

I find it helps to remind myself that I'm choosing to do something that I love. Win, lose or draw, I get to do what I love doing. There was a time when I was doing this for free. When I was fighting in the gym as an amateur, for free. Now I get to do it for money, for titles, for respect.

If I'm feeling pressure, it can help to remind myself that I chose to put myself in that situation. No one is forcing me to do this. If I suddenly had a change of heart on the way to the ring, no one could stop me from turning around and walking out of the building. No one is going to handcuff me and throw me into the ring. I chose every single step on the way to this fight, and at any stage I could have said: 'No, I'm done.' Once you appreciate that you're in control, and remind yourself that this is what you chose for yourself, that helps to reduce any pressure you might be feeling. Life isn't like a rollercoaster. It's not like you're locked in and you can't get off. At almost any moment, you can make a choice to take your life in a new direction.

Don't forget you're only under pressure, with people expecting a lot from you, because you've already accomplished so much in your life. You're good at what you do. You've performed well in the past and you can do it again now.

IN SHORT:

- Keep it simple and focus on what you need to do to succeed. That will stop you from over-complicating things and building them up in your mind.

- Tell yourself that this is one step on your journey – it's not the beginning or the end of your story.

- If you're doing something you love, and a job you chose, make sure you remind yourself of that. You're in control.

- You're only under pressure because you've already accomplished so much before. Remind yourself you're good at what you do.

What sacrifices will you make to achieve your dream?

I won't have sex in the days leading up a fight. That's not because I enjoy living like a monk. There's some science behind my abstinence: it helps to keep my testosterone levels high.

The only time I messed up, and had sex the day before a fight, I felt as though I'd lost my edge. Lying in bed, dangerous thoughts popped into my head: 'All is good in the world. I don't care whether I win, lose or draw.' That terrified me. That's not the mindset you want before stepping into the ring where your opponent will be trying to knock you out!

While I gathered myself, and still got the win, I told myself that I would never do that again. I'm willing to deny myself pleasure, and make whatever sacrifices it requires, to max out my potential as a boxer, which is why I haven't eaten any meat, or drunk any alcohol, since turning professional. I'm making sacrifices for my goals and, so far, the sacrifices have paid off.

The truth is, most people aren't willing to make all the sacrifices they need to achieve their dreams. That's because it's hard. You feel as though you're already sacrificing a lot. You tell yourself: 'I'm not doing this and that, so I think I'm going to allow myself that.' I understand. It's easy to think like that. Everyone wants to live a good life. We all want to live comfortably, we all want to enjoy ourselves. But if you're willing to make more sacrifices, that's going to separate you from everyone else who is chasing the same dream. If you have two people with the same ability, the difference could be who is willing to make the most sacrifices. It's the ones who are constantly pushing themselves who are going to go further, who can truly say they are doing everything to achieve their dreams.

It might help you to know that no one finds this easy. When I go to a party, I wish I could drink. But I know

If you have two
people with the
same ability,
the difference
could be who
is willing to
make the most
sacrifices.

that if I did have a beer, I would lose a day of training; I would be too hungover to function properly. I didn't want to get into the habit of going out drinking after winning a fight. When you go on a bender, it's hard to get back into training, and start getting into shape again for the next fight. Now I can go out until late, until 5am in the morning if I want to, and can still train the next day.

There are times when I've been tempted to have some meat, but I've stayed strong. Every time I'm out, it's quicker to grab chicken wings than it is to make avocados on toast when I get home, but I've stuck to it, and I'm proud of that.

If you truly believe, you're going to make the tough choices. You'll have the strength to say no to that beer, that party, that temptation. With sacrifice and dedication, you're making investments in your future. Every time you say no to going out, or drinking a pint, or whatever else it is that you're denying yourself, you're going to help yourself in the future. When you don't go to that party, you're putting that in the bank for later. It's about delayed gratification. You're thinking about the future rather than the present. You need to tell yourself: 'If I say no to this today,

I'm going to get a reward in the future that's several times bigger.'

It's OK to be selfish when it comes to your ambition. If you're going to succeed in life, you're going to have to be selfish. Selfish is a word that gets flung around a lot in arguments. I've had girlfriends tell me I'm selfish and self-obsessed because our relationship was dominated by my training and my preparation for the next fight. Selfish is seen as a negative word, as an insult. People don't usually like to be called selfish or to think of themselves as a selfish. But it's a lonely grind to the top and you'll only get there if you're selfish with your time and energy. If you give too much time and energy to others you're not going to have enough left for yourself and your dreams.

Being selfish presents challenges. You'll get complaints. People don't always like it when you say you're focused on your goal. At the end of a hard week's training, my friends, family or girlfriend might want to hang out at the weekend, but I can't meet them if that's going to stop me from going to bed on time, and being rested for my next training session.

Over time, the people around you will become accustomed to how dedicated you need to be

It's OK to be selfish when it comes to your ambition.

to reach your goals, and they should come to understand your selfishness is really sacrifice for your ambition.

If you're changing your behaviour because someone tells you that you're selfish, you won't be continuing with your mission. If you're completely transparent and open about the need to be selfish, and someone doesn't like that, that's not the sort of person you need around you on this journey. You need people who want you to succeed and support you in reaching your goals. You want people around you who allow you to be selfish, who recognise that putting yourself first is the only way that you're going to make your dreams come true. Don't let others knock you off track. Make sure you surround yourself with the right friends and supportive network. In return, I help and support my friends in whatever they are trying to accomplish with their own lives – this works both ways.

IN SHORT:

- If you're willing to make more sacrifices, that's going to separate you from everyone else chasing the same dream.

- Understand that no one finds this easy – feel proud of yourself if you can be strong and say no to temptations.

- Every time you say no, rather than thinking you're denying yourself some pleasure right now, instead tell yourself you're making an investment in your future.

- Be completely open and transparent about your need to be selfish, and explain that you're also denying yourself fun and pleasure.

Sleep your way to success

When I've had a good night's sleep - which means at least eight hours - my performance skyrockets. Sleep can have an enormous impact on how I train in the gym or in the ring: I'll feel sharper and have more energy. The better I'm sleeping, the better my preparation for a fight, and the better my chances of winning that fight. That's why, as I get down to the final weeks before a fight, I get even stricter with myself about going to bed on time and getting the sleep I need.

I feel so good after a decent night's sleep that it motivates me to keep on sticking to an early bedtime. When I'm preparing for a fight, I'll be out of bed at 7am most mornings, so if I'm going to get eight hours that means I need to be asleep by 11pm. To ensure that I'm getting the sleep that I need, and that my team know how I'm sleeping, I have apps that monitor and track my sleep patterns. Everyone knows how I'm sleeping and how I'm probably going to be feeling in training that day. If I'm staying up beyond midnight, I know that will affect my training in the morning, and I can't be doing that when I need to be in the best possible shape for a fight.

To ensure I recover between training sessions, I also have daytime naps. If you have the time, I recommend a short nap. Some days I get an hour's nap, and when I wake up I feel refreshed and ready for the rest of the day. When you're working hard, it's important to balance out your life with enough downtime and sleep. I know that if I lie down on the bed during the day, after a hard training session, my body is whispering to me: 'There you are, mate. Do what you need to do. You've been pushing yourself hard, and you get so many aches and soreness. It's time to sleep.'

It's important that you give yourself the best chance of getting a good night's sleep. Look at your bedroom set up - can you make it a better place to sleep? Do you have lights that you can get rid of, or could you

It's important that you give yourself the best chance of getting a good night's sleep. Look at your bedroom set up – can you make it a better place to sleep?

block out the streetlights outside your window to make it darker? Try not to take your phone to bed with you. I also think about my caffeine intake. You're unlikely to sleep well if you have a coffee just before you go to bed; don't do it.

IN SHORT:

- If you get enough sleep, you'll have more energy and feel sharper, and you'll perform better (that's true whether you're sitting at a desk or you're in a boxing ring).

- Be strict with yourself about going to bed on time and try to make time for a nap.

- Make sure you have a comfortable bed, and don't drink coffee late at night.

Have faith

Before a fight, I'll pray for my opponent as well as for myself. While I want to win, I don't want to damage someone for life. I'm praying for the safety of myself and my opponent, that we're both going to be OK when we walk out of the ring. What I don't do is pray to God that I knock someone out. After all, we're talking about violence here.

I pray for mental fortitude, that I can demonstrate what I've been working on in training, and that I make my family proud. I also pray that I make myself proud, as the one thing I don't want is to be thinking after the fight that I could have done things differently, and that I didn't show what I was capable of.

I pray throughout camp, and then on the day of a fight I might pray several times. Just before I leave my hotel room to go to the arena, that's when it gets deeper as you might not have another opportunity to do a longer prayer before getting into the ring. Sometimes I'll pray just before I leave my dressing room. I'll close my eyes and say a few words that are just between me and God.

When I was in school, I was ashamed of my African first name, Ikechukwu, but then my parents told me that it means 'God's power', which is a fitting name for a boxer. They gave me that name because I was born premature. I was put into an incubator for weeks and no one was sure whether I would survive. But I did.

I believe my faith has helped my boxing and also my life generally. My faith helps me to remember that there's a purpose to life, and to keep working at being an all-round better person. Everyone's definition of a good person is different, but I think it means treating others how you want to be treated. Faith helps me remember this simple rule for life.

I once tweeted that it was for God to 'grant me the persistence and perseverance to conquer myself and then the world'. I believe God is there to help you with that sort of stuff. You can only ask God for the power to do what's possible, within your own capabilities. I'm asking God for me to be strong of heart and mind to push. I know I can win fights. God can't give you the power to do something that isn't within you already.

If you've got a task in front of you that's difficult, ask for strength and persistence so you can do that. There are always going to be temptations and challenges. You need to find the strength of character to face them and make the right choices for you.

Faith also lets you face up to the mistakes you've made. Faith helps you to work hard in the future.

I'm not much of a churchgoer at the moment. It's a tough one because what I do is very violent. Some people will say that it's not right for boxers to be going to church. Until I've finished with my combat, I'm going to keep my relationship with God going on my own.

If I post something on social media saying that I've just had a hard session in camp and I'm feeling tired, my mum might see that and send me a prayer. She also prays for me. She prays for God's power and strength to be put on me and that I don't shake or falter.

You might not share my beliefs, and that's OK. Faith comes in many forms. For me, prayer to God is a powerful way to sort through my thoughts and feelings and focus my positive energy on my purpose.

You might not share my beliefs, and that's OK. Faith comes in many forms. For me, prayer to God is a powerful way to sort through my thoughts and feelings and focus my positive energy on my purpose.

It helps me dig deep and gives me strength. There is way more going on than any of us understand or can explain, and there are bigger things out there than us. Having faith might help you put the challenges in your life into perspective and help you reach beyond them to find the power already inside of you. If you're not religious, you could also try meditation and mindfulness to clear and focus your mind.

IN SHORT:

- Faith can help you conquer yourself and then the world.

- Faith can be a motivational force.

- You don't have to go to church to have faith.

- For those who don't have a religious faith, meditation and mindfulness could help to give you clarity and focus.

Be curious: it will give you power

I'm a level beyond curious; I'm inquisitive. I'll keep asking questions because I want to know everything. The more information you have, the more power you have. That's true inside and outside a boxing ring.

When I'm interested in a subject, I dive right in. I'm going deep. I'll start with online research and watching any YouTube videos that are going to add to my knowledge, and I'll find the right people to speak to and then ask them lots of questions. While I don't care about gossip, and I'm never nosy about what's going on in people's private lives, I go all in when I want to add to my knowledge. If you want to improve at anything, the fastest way of doing that is to find an expert and then ask them lots of questions.

For a while, my obsession was learning everything about fighting southpaws, or left-handed boxers. I had lost to a southpaw as an amateur. I had the physicality, the work ethic and the talent to beat him, so what else did I need to know about fighting a southpaw? I researched all the best southpaws in the world, and watched videos of their fights. Then I found which boxers had beaten them, and how they had gone about it. I watched all their fights, too.

When you're fighting a southpaw, you have to understand exactly how their positioning differs from other boxers, and also that punches are going to be coming in from different angles. You need to know about physics and movement if you're going to appreciate what's happening in the ring. I talked to my coach, asked him questions that could help me with the best strategy against a southpaw. I was researching where to stand, how to move, and what I should and shouldn't be doing. Don't be afraid to ask others for advice; you don't have to know everything. Look to the experts and those with experience in your life and ask them for help.

It's not enough to be asking questions; you also need to be listening carefully to the answers and then putting that into practice.

I'm not asking questions just to know, and because I want that knowledge for its own sake. This isn't theoretical. I'm asking questions because I want to do something, and because I want to apply that knowledge. It's not enough to be asking questions; you also need to be listening carefully to the answers and then putting that into practice.

Sometimes people around me tell me to slow down, and to take something one step at a time, but that's because as soon as I learn how to do something I want to do it straightaway. Asking questions and then immediately acting on that information lets you quickly find out your capabilities and limitations. The expert you're speaking to might suggest that you do something and that makes you realise that you can't do it today. Being curious teaches you to work on something.

IN SHORT:

- The more information you have, the more power you have, so keep on asking lots of questions.

- If you're looking for fast improvements, find an expert and ask them lots of questions.

- Asking questions isn't enough – you also have to listen to the answers and put that into practice.

- Being curious lets you quickly find out your capabilities and limitations.

PART 4
SUCCESS STORY

Can you handle your initial success? How you answer that question could determine whether you're successful in the long term or burn out fast. In this fourth and final section, I want to share some advice on how to think and behave when things are going well for you, including how you should be proud on the inside and humble on the outside. It's crucial to celebrate those successes, but you also need to cope with other people's jealousies, and avoid being distracted by your personal life. Make sure your voice is heard and that you build your brand, but don't become obsessed with body image and having Instagram abs. And what now? What's the next challenge? Are you ready for your future?

Proud on the inside, humble on the outside

In my mind, there's no contradiction between pride and humility. You can be both proud and humble at the same time. You can feel proud of yourself and what you've accomplished through hard work but you don't need to seek praise or public acknowledgement for your achievements.

I'm not going to lie – I enjoy some of the attention I get. I like being asked for pictures when I'm out. But I don't do what I do for others' validation, for public glory; I do it for me.

If you allow pride to take over your life, and it's dictating every situation, you can be sure it's eventually going to drag you down. That's how I lived my life as a teenager. I was either full of pride or, and this was much more problematic, feeling a loss of pride - or feeling like someone had disrespected me. If you let pride rule your life, you'll spend too much time thinking about and reacting to the small things, all the stuff that doesn't really matter.

I can now see how an excess of pride doesn't make me more of a man. If anything, it made me less of a man, and my pride came from feeling insecure. If I'm honest, I was getting upset over some really minor stuff, and I know I shouldn't have made a big deal out of things.

I know it's annoying, for example, in a bar or a club when someone steps on your shoe or spills your drink, and they then don't say sorry, and you might feel your pride has been hurt. You're probably drunk but you should just ignore the guy or speak to him in a less aggressive tone, but you just can't help yourself. There was a time when my friends and I were getting into fights in clubs every other week, and that was because we let pride take over. Every situation, however small, would escalate and we would find ourselves fighting again.

We talked about the importance of standing up for yourself earlier (see page 47), and I would urge you not to let anyone walk all over you. But you mustn't go to the other extreme where you're constantly reacting to small losses of pride. Back then, I wasn't good at the back and forth of conversation, and if someone made a joke, I would be thinking to myself: 'I'm going to have to fight him.' It was as if I didn't have a choice: I would then try to engineer a fight, maybe provoke him or somehow make sure it got heated. I think I even enjoyed it, which sounds stupid now.

This was just before I got into boxing. The amount of fighting over spilled drinks was getting out of hand, and my friendship group agreed we needed to do something about it. From then on, we decided we would go out of our way to soothe situations. We would always be ready to say sorry, and to put our hands up in apology, rather than get into yet another altercation. That meant we could have a night out without a fight, and we found that we didn't feel like we were lesser men because we didn't want to punch someone over a spilled lager. I just wish that I had realised sooner that I didn't have to carry myself in a certain way. That would have saved me a lot of time, effort and aggravation.

Ask any young man about the fights he's had in nightclubs and they'll almost all be based on nothing. That's pride getting the better of the man. Road rage is also usually about pride. Someone has cut you up at the lights or kept you waiting for ten seconds and you feel slighted. You can't deal with it and there's a flash of anger. You're thinking about ramming the other guy's car. There's a flaw in many human beings that makes them over-react in situations like that, even in a quiet office. Maybe someone just casually asked you to make him a cup of tea, as he thought you were going to the office kitchen, and you explode because you think that's beneath you.

If you feel as though pride keeps taking over, it's because you feel a constant need to prove yourself. You need to find a way of feeling more comfortable in yourself, and realising that you're not defined by others and how they treat you.

In general, pride is a problem for people who have done less with their lives so far, when they've got less to be proud of. If you're one of those people who is obsessing over the small stuff, take a moment to consider what you've done so far, what you've

You need to find
a way of feeling
more comfortable
in yourself, and
realising that
you're not defined
by others and how
they treat you.

got going for you, and what you want to achieve – remember your ambition, refocus, and channel your energy into that, not the small stuff. You'll no longer feel the constant need to prove yourself. That will help you to be proud on the inside, humble on the outside.

IN SHORT:

- If you're more comfortable in yourself, you'll realise you're not defined by others and how they treat you.

- Don't feel as though you have to constantly prove yourself.

- Recognise that you're getting upset about minor stuff – let it go and put your energy into pursuing your ambition.

Body image: why a six-pack won't make you happy

When you're as fat as I was as a teenager, it eats away at you, it devours you, it possibly even disgusts you. My belly was making me have dark, dangerous thoughts. I was standing naked in front of a bathroom mirror, grabbing great, soft, generous handfuls of belly fat, and thinking I should just rip my stomach from my body.

In my disturbed teenage mind, that would give me what I had always craved: a six-pack. Being young, stupid and unhappy, there was an even more extreme option. I'd read about liposuction and what a surgeon's blade could do, and now I was asking myself whether I should cut myself in the bathroom with a kitchen knife, and let the fat, and all my problems, ooze to the floor. Fat can turn you mad. It's the shame and the daily humiliation. The self-loathing. I'd had years of cruel comments about my weight – and of bullies whipping up my T-shirt so I would 'flash' my belly to the class – but the jibes that particular day had taken me somewhere new, to a dark place where I wanted to carve and mutilate my body. I was trying to lose weight, but it just wasn't happening for me, because I knew nothing about a healthy diet.

At a time when stabbings were commonplace in London, here I was thinking of taking a knife to myself. While I didn't act on that thought – I couldn't quite bring myself to slice into my belly – I stayed angry, frustrated and upset. I cried that day.

Having been to both extremes – as an elite boxer I've now got what some might describe as 'Instagram abs' – I feel as though I've got something to say about body image. If you're looking in the mirror right now and hating what you see, I know what that's like: I've been there. I can assure you that there's a way out of this situation, that you can change how you feel about your body and yourself.

At my heaviest, I was nineteen stone, which was more than five stone overweight for my height. That's waddle-down-the-street fat. But the truth is that I'd probably been overweight from the age of six or seven. I was always a fat kid. I don't want to blame my mother but, growing up in a home with African heritage, we never wasted any food. My mother gave me and my younger brother big portions, and even then nothing ever went uneaten. If there was any leftover plantain, or whatever else was on the table that day, I would eat it.

By the time I was in secondary school, I was eating six meals a day. I would have my first breakfast at home, and then go to a club at school for my second. I would never leave the canteen during lunch break, always sticking around until seconds were served, or even thirds if apple crumble was on the menu. Not once did I leave the canteen to play with the other kids outside. That gave me the time to have my two lunches. After getting home from school, and before my mum returned, I would cook myself some eggy bread, and then later I would eat the dinner she prepared.

In between my six meals, I was gorging on sweets. People joke about having a sweet tooth, but I think I must have been addicted to sugar. I ate lots of sweets. I loved all sweets and chocolates. If I suddenly had £10 in my pocket, I would spend all that money on the sweetest of sugar highs. Why did I do that to myself? That wasn't the question I was asking myself. It was: why wouldn't I spend all my money on sweets? Hamburgers were another vice. As a teenager, I ate a lot of Big Macs. Working in McDonald's as a teenager, I was hardly going to reduce my burger habit.

No one had ever taught me about nutrition or moderation. I had got to my late teens without knowing what a healthy diet looked like, and I'm sure I'm not alone in that. If you feel as though you're clueless on diet and health, you need to do some reading. Only then will you have the information you need to change your body.

In other chapters, I write about why I'm a teetotal vegan, why I haven't touched meat and alcohol as a boxer – this is what works for me.

As a child and then as a teenager, I was about as far from being an athlete as you can imagine. Back then, I couldn't do a lap of the park. After just a few metres,

I would be huffing and puffing while my friends disappeared into the distance. But being fat isn't just a physical problem; it's also a mental issue. Being fat can destroy your confidence. As much as I wanted a girlfriend, I had no confidence around girls. Even if a girl showed some interest in me, I didn't believe them. How could she possibly like someone as chubby as me? But this wasn't just about girls; I had little to no confidence in almost any situation.

As I said, being fat eats away at you. That was the reason I took up boxing in the first place – to burn some fat. This was before Anthony Joshua's success at the 2012 London Games inspired me to want to become an Olympian. For a couple of years before the London Olympics, I wasn't thinking about medals, belts, money and fame. My motivation was losing my belly, of no longer always being the heaviest guy in the room. If you need to lose weight, you could think about joining a boxing gym. Or find another sport – any sport – that's going to get you moving regularly and help you to transform your body.

As a boxer, your body is always being weighed, analysed, scrutinised. At the pre-fight weigh-in, you step on the scales in public, and feel even more exposed in the ring when you're naked from the waist up. You don't get to hide away under a baggy T-shirt. I'm in excellent shape as a boxer – I'm as fit and as strong as I've ever been.

Losing all my teenage fat has undoubtedly changed how I feel about myself. It's crazy how much my body has changed, and how much confidence I have now that I'm no longer so heavy. I'll sometimes bump into old school friends who I haven't seen for years and they're shocked at my transformation. They just say: 'Wow.'

But I'm going to let you in on a secret: most of the time, I don't actually have a six-pack. I'm one of the fittest people on the planet, part of the one per cent, and yet I only look that ripped on the day of a fight and when I'm doing high-intensity training in my fight camp. In short, when I'm pushing my body to the limit. Most of the photographs of me online were taken in the ring. Those are the images that stick with people. The rest of the time, when I don't have a fight coming up, my abs aren't so defined. Between fights, I'm enjoying my food – my biggest monthly spend is probably Uber Eats – and that's fine. I know that when a fight is approaching, I have the discipline to clean up my diet and stop snacking on the American pancakes and the occasional bags of Haribo.

I know a lot of men feel pressure to look a certain way – with a flat, hard stomach like a *Love Island* contestant. That aesthetic is not an ideal to aspire to. I know from my own experience how unrealistic it is. Yes, it's possible to look like that with a lot of hard work and deprivation, but it's also close to impossible to sustain that look for very long.

What people who look like that don't tell you is that you only look like that if you go to the gym twice a day, and have a very controlled diet. For some, their abs are their job. Many men with a six-pack aren't happy. They're hungry. Most people with regular jobs simply don't have the time or the energy to have a body like that. I want you to focus on your health rather than body image. You wouldn't want to be as heavy and as unhappy as I was growing up, but at the same time you can make yourself just as miserable aiming for impossibly sculpted abs.

If you have a regular job, and if you eat healthily, and keep active, you'll have a healthy body. And I think that should be celebrated. Don't be hard on yourself if you're not ripped and you don't have abs.

The media is only interested in showing us sculpted bodies. My advice is to be healthy and happy. If you're healthy, you'll learn to love your body when you stand in front of a mirror.

Society needs to be having a conversation about what an attractive man or woman looks like. I feel as though healthy bodies aren't appreciated any more. The media is only interested in showing us sculpted bodies. My advice is to be healthy and happy. If you're healthy, you'll learn to love your body when you stand in front of a mirror.

IN SHORT:

- Having a six-pack isn't going to make you feel happy or fulfilled – try to be healthy rather than aspiring to have Instagram abs.

- If you hate your reflection, there's a way to change how you feel about your body and yourself.

- If you don't know much, or anything, about diet and nutrition, you need to educate yourself.

- You also need to move your body more. Join a boxing gym, or find a sport that you enjoy doing, that's going to help you get in shape.

Celebrate your successes

Other boxers might go on benders after winning a fight. As I don't drink, I reward myself in other ways – with a giant bag of sweets, chocolates and cakes, like something out of Willy Wonka's factory.

Before the fight, I'll fill that bag with high-quality chocolates, and all the sweet stuff that I had been denying myself for months to get in shape. I'll tell myself that the bag is there waiting for me on the other side of the fight, once I've knocked the other guy out. One of my friends will bring the bag to his hotel room, and then he'll fetch it after the fight. Eating sweets has become my post-fight ritual.

I feel as though it's important to celebrate your successes, and you should acknowledge to yourself that you've achieved your goals. But you need to be careful that how you celebrate success doesn't damage your long-term ambition or become destructive to your life. I stopped drinking because that was potentially damaging my future prospects.

The winning feeling doesn't last as long as you might think. I'm certainly not in a state of joy and euphoria for days and weeks afterwards – and sometimes I just feel relief. And I would say to you, don't get too caught up on that one success. Celebrate your achievement and then get back to work, refocus, graft.

Every single time I win, after the celebration I think: 'What's next? What's the next goal that I want to achieve?' I want to be ticking those boxes. You win one day and there's always another potential win to start thinking about and preparing for – stay hungry.

IN SHORT:

- Celebrate your successes as you need to acknowledge to yourself that you've achieved your goal.

- However, don't overdo the celebrations if that's going to harm your future prospects.

- It's OK if you feel relief rather than joy when you accomplish a goal.

- While you're celebrating, you might instantly start asking yourself, 'What's next?', and thinking about future challenges.

Coping with other people's jealousies

The cynical amongst you might think that most of the trash-talking between boxers is just showbusiness. That they are just empty, scripted words to sell fights. But that's not my experience of the fight game.

Nine times out of ten when a boxer says something cutting to another boxer it's because he genuinely doesn't like his opponent. He means what he says. When we're talking trash, we're not pretending to dislike each other. That trash is real. Every time I've had a go at another boxer it's because I've been feuding with him, not because my promoter put me up to it.

I've had a few feuds in my career and every time they've stemmed from jealousy. I talked earlier in the book about how to stop yourself being jealous of others and how it's not going to get you anywhere (see pages 39–46). Here I want to tell you what it's been like to have been on the other side of that, and to have dealt with other boxers' professional jealousies.

'British Beef' was how one of my fights was promoted. Other British boxers, especially those in London, resented me as soon as I turned professional. They had some beef with me because they had put in years of work and still had no profile or television dates. But, because I had been an Olympian, I turned professional and immediately had sponsors and endorsement deals. There was massive fanfare when I turned pro, as I was the first of the 2016 Olympians to do so, and then I got my first knock-out as a professional and the clip went everywhere on social media. That was a crazy, exciting time for me. If you're doing exciting things in your life, it's almost inevitable that others will be jealous of you. Other people's jealousy is a sign that you're on the right track.

It helps to understand why others are jealous of you; you'll have an explanation for why they're behaving as they are around you. It was clear that the other boxers weren't happy with their situation and felt as though they deserved to be in my position instead. They weren't focusing on their own goals and were too caught up in wasting energy on me.

One opponent even paid to place a spoof advert in a newspaper saying that I would be looking for work after he knocked me out. That was funny. But the problem for him was that when you do something like that and lose, you look very stupid.

If I'm honest, I liked some of the energy and edge that came from my jealous opponents. I channelled the energy into training that tiny bit harder. I would tell myself: 'I'm not losing to that guy – I just can't let him win.'

Don't get bogged down with petty squabbles; keep your sights on your mission. For some of my opponents, their pinnacle is to fight me – they're not going to get any better than that. For me, fighting and beating those guys was just a small step on the way to much greater things. To me, my opponents are just steps to get to where I wanted to be. Their jealousies didn't stop me on my mission and other people's jealousies should never stop you either.

IN SHORT:

- It always helps to deal with other people's jealousies if you can understand why they feel that way towards you.

- If you're successful, it's inevitable that others will be jealous of you. It's a sign that you're on the right track.

- If a feud develops out of their jealousy, you can use it to your advantage as it might bring extra energy that's going to help you push towards your own ambitions.

- Don't be dragged down to their level – stick to your mission.

Let your family inspire you

My mum isn't ringside for my fights, and I wouldn't want her there either. Anything can happen in boxing, and I think it's just too intense for her to watch me live, even if I'm the one knocking people out. It's better if she's at home in front of her TV, watching my fight on delay in the knowledge that I've already won.

In the beginning, my mum wasn't happy with the idea of her son being a boxer. She worried about me getting hurt, and used to talk about boxers biting each other's ears off, as she had heard about the time Mike Tyson took a chunk out of Evander Holyfield. 'Why,' she asked, 'would you want to be a boxer?'

But eventually Mum came around to the idea. She saw how I was losing weight and the discipline I got from it. Training in the gym was also keeping me away from gangs in the area, so she could see the positives. As time went on, Mum realised I was winning fights and making progress, and she's now my number one fan.

My family have always been at the heart of my story. It would have been difficult for me to have achieved what I did without my family, who supported me when I quit McDonald's to commit to boxing. They have helped to shape me into the person I am today. I always give them the credit for that. One lesson I learned from my parents was the importance of working hard. Mum and Dad were in their mid-twenties when they came to Britain from Nigeria. They didn't have much when they arrived and I'm proud of how they invested in themselves and worked hard to better their lives and also their children's lives.

Mum's first job in Britain was a cleaner. She used to work on an estate that was known for gang violence and we used to go there with her. From there, she worked her way up to porter, and then went to college and university, getting the education to become a social worker. It was a similar story with my dad, who was a taxi driver when he first came to

Britain, and then worked a few other jobs, doing a little bit of this and a little bit of that, before studying for a law degree.

I've told Mum and Dad how the example of their hard work has allowed me to do what I do. I've told them I'm proud of them and I've also shown my gratitude with my actions, helping them to make their lives more comfortable. They could easily have done nothing, but they pushed to elevate themselves, and that will always be an inspiration to me.

Family can help to motivate you. When you've got a family that you want to take care of, that will give you an extra push. I want to help my family, including my future kids, to have a better life. If your family are behind you from the start, that's great, and you'll want to show them that they were right to believe in you. But if your family aren't on board with your dream in the early days, as my mum wasn't with my boxing, that doesn't mean that you should stop doing something. Your family want what's best for you, but they don't always know what's best, and you can change their mind with the progress and success you have. If my family continue to inspire me, I think I also inspire them now as I'm pushing to elevate myself.

I speak to my mum several times a week, and I see a lot of her as she makes food for me. I probably speak to my dad once a week. Family is a great support system when things aren't going your way. And when you're achieving great things, family will help to ground you. They'll remind you of where you came from, and help you to stay humble.

Everyone's story is different and I'm aware, of course, that not everyone has a solid family life. That's especially true of some boxers, who have had a hard upbringing and who might have got into the sport to escape what was going on at home or on the streets. But 'family' doesn't have to mean blood relatives; you can see a close circle of old friends as your family.

IN SHORT:

- Take inspiration from your family and also try to inspire them.

- Let family motivate you to push harder for your dreams.

- Your family want what's best for you, but they don't always know what's best for you - don't give up on your ambition just because your family aren't on board from the beginning.

- If you start to have some success, family will keep you grounded and remind you where you came from.

Make your voice heard

Twice within twenty minutes, I was stopped and searched by the police. That must have been some kind of record, even for Hackney.

The second time officers blocked me on the street, I handed them the slip of paper from the first encounter, which had the time of the search on it. The ink was so fresh on that form that it would have smudged in our hands. But the police wouldn't just let me walk on and continue with my day. They said I could have picked up something – I think they were hinting at a knife or drugs, perhaps – during those twenty minutes between searches. Just like the first time, I had nothing on me. I wasn't a gangster. But the police just wouldn't leave me alone that day. Walking home from school, I was stopped and searched for a third time.

I hated it. Being stopped and searched is more than annoying: it's humiliating, invasive and deeply upsetting. But the saddest part of all was that I also became conditioned to it. Every young black man in London did, because it happened so often. Being targeted by the police was just a part of life for a black teenager. I must have had at least a hundred stop-and-searches. I would tell myself: 'OK, this is just to be expected. I'm a young black man and I'm going to be targeted by the police, sometimes even two or three times a day.'

As you get older as a black male, you go from wondering whether you're going to be stopped and searched while on foot to thinking about whether you'll be pulled over when driving. I'm in my late twenties now and whenever I see a police car I wonder whether I'm about to be pulled over.

That has happened to me since I became a professional boxer. I asked the police why they had been so suspicious of me and they said that usually people driving cars like mine – especially when it was men of my age – were involved in gang activities. Apparently I was driving through an area where the gangs were active. They didn't say that it was because

I was black, but they didn't have to: I knew exactly what was going on when the lights started flashing. It's distressing, of course, but we've become accustomed to it. Through my experience, I'm conditioned to how many of the institutions in Britain, such as the police, keep black people down.

I think people had become conditioned to seeing police brutality against black people. Videos would appear on the newsfeeds of me and my friends and they were always painful to watch, but we would say to ourselves: 'Oh, there's another one.' Within days, there would be another. But when the video emerged of the killing of George Floyd in the United States in 2020, that was different. As a black man, you watched someone who looked like you, who actually could have been you, dying on the street.

If you're not living that life, it can be difficult to understand what it's like being black. But that video raised awareness among all races of what black people are dealing with every day.

I watched as a police officer's knee pushed down on George's neck, and as George repeatedly called out, 'I can't breathe'. That provoked so many emotions in me: anger, frustration, helplessness and empathy. I

Speak out
and you'll
give yourself,
or someone
else, the best
chance of
turning their
dreams into
reality.

felt pain. The violence against black people has been continuous and senseless, and comes from a very dark place. But I was encouraged by the reaction, and how George Floyd's death sparked such a big civil rights movement around the world. I went to two Black Lives Matter protests in London, and it was great to see people of all races standing together and saying it was time for change.

I urge you to make your voice heard and to push for change. Only then, when there's full equality, will black people have the same opportunities. Speak out and you'll give yourself, or someone else, the best chance of turning their dreams into reality.

Through my boxing, I now have a platform to speak out. But everyone can make themselves heard. You mustn't be afraid. Change will only happen if people of all skin colours continue to speak out and there are more eyes on the issues that are affecting black people and other ethnic minorities in Britain, America and across the world. I'm hopeful because people of all races are now wise to a lot of stuff that previously they didn't know about.

I want my future kids to feel more comfortable going about their lives than I did. I don't want them to worry about being targeted by the police, or being pulled over because they might be driving an expensive car. I don't want them to feel fear whenever they see a policeman approaching.

Much of the racism that I encounter in Britain today is subtle. I'll be walking around a clothes shop in a smart part of town, and I can sense that a shop assistant is following me. Then, after a minute or so, someone will say to me: 'Are you alright? Do you need anything?' But I've worked in retail before and I know what's really happening. They're sending me a message: 'We're watching you.'

That's the racism that you can't prove, because it's so subtle. There's an institutional racism in Britain. Friends apply for jobs and worry that they won't get asked for an interview because of their surnames, because they sound black. People are genuinely worried about putting a name like Okolie on their application form. You can't prove whether you really missed out on that job because of the colour of your skin but it's always in the back of your mind.

A final thought: police officers are human beings. Like everyone else, they have the media telling them that black boys are gangsters. That's the stereotype that the media is always pushing. People look at a group of black boys and wonder whether they're gangsters. People are intimidated when they see black boys on the streets when they wouldn't be scared by a group of white boys. The media has power to change this perception.

I haven't been stopped by the police for a while now. Maybe the police are still stopping and searching black teenagers as much as they did when I was that age, but I'm just a little older now. Or maybe change is happening. I'm hopeful now.

IN SHORT:

- Don't be afraid to speak out – make your voice heard.

- Change will only happen if people of all skin colours continue to speak out against racism and injustice.

- Equality is only possible if we stop the stereotype of black boys being gangsters.

Don't let your personal life distract you

Mentally and emotionally, I was all over the place. I had just broken up with my girlfriend; I was sad and upset. She was a rapper and it felt as though they kept on playing her music on the radio. I would be in the gym – maybe on the treadmill or hitting the bag – when one of her tracks would start and I would have to stop what I was doing and refocus. It was like the DJs were tormenting me – for a while it felt as though I couldn't go a day without hearing my ex's voice.

And yet, for all the intense emotions that I was feeling – I was also dealing with a family problem that was a real burden – I managed to keep it together. While I might have been all over the place outside the gym and the ring, I was committed and focused when I needed to be. I had a fight to prime myself for and I wouldn't allow myself to be off my game. Throughout my career, I've always ensured my personal life doesn't have a negative impact on my dreams and ambitions, and that I've been totally professional. I'm on a mission in my career, and I'm not going to allow heartbreak or any other drama in my personal life to distract me. Those songs on the radio didn't throw me off for long. I was soon fully focused again.

I'm fortunate as a boxer. Boxing is such a high pressure and dangerous sport that it's easy to prioritise and to ensure that I don't lose my focus. When I go to the gym, the people there don't care about my break-up, and my opponent certainly won't care about my girl problems, or whatever else is going on in my life.

But I know there's a difference between doing 100 push-ups and just getting through them and doing 100 push-ups with intent. If you're going to get the best out of yourself, your mind must be fully there.

If something's going on in my personal life, I'll say to myself before every session: 'Put everything you have into this and then you can go back to being sad or whatever else afterwards. But for this hour and a half, put all your energy and focus into getting ready for your fight.'

Away from work, you can't hide from the drama in your personal life, and you're going to have to deal with it. But you can decide whether it's going to stop you from giving your all in your professional life. If you have a big work goal in your life that you can put your energy into, that stops you from thinking too much about the drama in your personal life.

If you're ambitious, you need to make sure you're with someone who's going to help you achieve those dreams. Relationships can be hard if you allow them to be, and if you choose the wrong person. I feel as though it's important to maintain who you are outside that relationship.

The sad times can distract you, but so can the good times. If you're in a new relationship, and you're in that stage when you feel as though you want to spend all your time with that person, you have to be wary of that.

I know that if I dedicate myself to boxing, it will reward me. It must be the only thing I can say that about. With family, you can do everything right in your opinion and it still doesn't work out. With a relationship, you can give them everything you think the other person wants and needs, and it still doesn't work out. Ultimately, you can still love your partner and love your family. But that thing you're doing, that dream you're working towards, that's going to bring you something. That's yours. No one can take that away from you. Whatever you put in you take out. If you keep focused, and don't let anything distract you, you're going to be rewarded for that.

IN SHORT:

- Keep an eye on the big picture – even when you've got drama in your personal life, you need to stay fully focused on your dreams.

- Outside work, you can't hide from your personal problems, but when it's time to work you need to be fully focused.

- Having a dream or ambition can help to distract you from heartbreak or other personal problems – rather than the other way around.

- Be careful who you get together with – and don't be afraid to walk away if a relationship is distracting you from your ambitions.

- If you dedicate yourself to your dreams, you'll be rewarded. You can't always say that about your relationships and your family.

Special sauce: develop your personal brand

As it says on my fight shorts, I'm 'The Sauce'. My nickname means something in urban culture - that I've got swagger and edge, that I've got a different kind of energy to most people. But that's not how I became 'The Sauce'. You'll know by now that McDonald's is a big part of my story, and my nickname is a reference to fast food, and a reminder of my time flipping burgers and being hooked on Big Macs.

It goes back to a press conference before my professional debut when I compared boxing to a burger. I likened whether or not you can win a fight to the protein patty - that's the most important element, the bit in the middle that everything else is built around. There are other elements to being a boxer, such as your interaction with fans – they could be the bun, the salad and the slice of cheese. And then on top of the patty there's your special sauce, which is your charisma or energy.

My management team must have liked my burger story because they had 'The Sauce' added to my shorts in time for my first fight. I've had that nickname on my shorts ever since. Getting a nickname so early on in my career, before I'd even had my first fight as a pro, only helped me to build my brand.

Working with Eddie Hearn, who's the biggest boxing promoter in the world, I've learned plenty about the importance of branding. He keeps everything fresh and modern – he's always coming up with new ideas to promote his champions. In any industry, you want people to buy into you and your story. In boxing, that means that they want you to win, that they feel invested in you. It's all about how many people are aware of your fight, how many eyes are on you, and ultimately who cares whether you win or lose? Building my personal brand means I have more people watching my fights, and also creates endorsement opportunities.

Building a brand isn't about being a fake. It's about showing people the real you. That should always be enough. You need to be authentic if you want to build a brand that lasts. Don't try to create a fake persona, and pretend you're someone you're not, as eventually people will see through that.

For me that means I'm not going to create a fake feud with another boxer, and say things I don't mean, just to push my brand, I'm not going to endorse something I don't believe in, or say something just to get more headlines or followers. I also won't do projects that don't sit right.

I'm not telling you that your social media following is the most important thing to focus on. And I am not saying that you need to be famous to have a good life. I'm suggesting to stay true to yourself, think about what you want to achieve, what you believe is right, and live by that, communicate that in everything you do. Build the right reputation that represents who you really are and don't try to be anyone else because that will just complicate your mission and won't help you to succeed.

Your personal brand should reflect the reality of who you are. I'm comfortable being 'The Sauce' because I

Build the right reputation that represents who you really are and don't try to be anyone else because that will just complicate your mission and won't help you to succeed.

do have swagger and energy and I am also proud of where I have come from; that moment in McDonald's changed my life and is part of who I am. What you see is what you get.

IN SHORT:

- If you have a personal brand, it helps people to buy into you and your story.

- Be authentic. Creating a brand isn't about being fake – it's about showing people the real you.

- When you're going through adversity, you'll reveal your true character and people will see whether your brand is a reflection of the real you.

Are you ready for your future?

I like the idea of going full circle with McDonald's. By the time I'm thirty, I want to own a couple of McDonald's franchises. Then I'll be circling back to my past, and to the moment – working in the McDonald's in Victoria Station during the London 2012 Olympic Games – that I was inspired to become a boxer.

I have strong memories of working in McDonald's. I also still have the badge I had to wear in the station. Back then, I could only dream about working my way up to manager and then possibly running my own McDonald's; now I can think about owning a couple.

I'm hoping, as a vegan, that I could have vegan options on the menus of my McDonald's restaurants. While these are the best days of my life as a boxer, it's important to appreciate that my time as an athlete is limited and that I need to have a plan for the future and for my life after boxing. As I wrote in a previous chapter, you need to have a strategy. You need one for the long term as well as the short term.

I'm in my late twenties now and I should have done enough as a boxer by my mid-thirties. I want to keep going until I feel as though I'm losing my speed and my strength. I know how I feel when I'm in a boxing ring now; I feel near enough invincible. If I started to lose that shine, that's when I would walk away. If it starts to feel hard in sparring, and I know the guy's not that good, that's when I'll hang it up.

IN SHORT:

- You might not be able to carry on doing what you're doing for the rest of your career – it would help to have a vision for what you might do next.

- You should know when it's time to move on to your next challenge.

CONCLUSION

I don't want this to be a book that you read once and never pick up again. I'm hoping that *Dare to Change Your Life* is a book that you can turn to again and again when you're looking for inspiration, guidance and encouragement, and when you're going through dark times or good times. I know Anthony Joshua appreciates it when I tell him how he shaped my life, and I would love to hear your stories, so please get in touch over social media, on Twitter or Instagram, or through AJ's management company, 258 Management. I dared to change my life, and I would be so happy if I could help you change yours too.

INDEX

ACKNOWLEDGEMENTS

I would like to thank Anthony Joshua, Shane McGuigan, Eddie Hearn, Will Harvey, Duncan Ogilvie, Fred Mellor, Freddie Cunningham, Scott Robinson, Fearne Cotton, Mark Hodgkinson, Laura Higginson, Ellie Crisp, Anna Bowers, Donna Hillyer, Loulou Clark, Gurdas Singh, Nick Walters, David Luxton, Henry Okolie, and Mum and Dad.